World War 1

A Captivating Guide to the First World War, Including Battle Stories from the Eastern and Western Front and How the Treaty of Versailles in 1919 Impacted the Rise of Nazi Germany

Free Bonus from Captivating History (Available for a Limited time)

Hi History Lovers!

Now you have a chance to join our exclusive history list so you can get your first history ebook for free as well as discounts and a potential to get more history books for free! Simply visit the link below to join.

Captivatinghistory.com/ebook

Also, make sure to follow us on Facebook, Twitter and Youtube by searching for Captivating History.

Timeline of Significant Events in the First World War

1914

June 28: Assassination of Franz Ferdinand

July 28: The Austro-Hungarian Empire declares war on Serbia

Germany immediately allies itself with the Austro-Hungarian Empire and declares war on Serbia

Russia, in accordance with its alliance with Serbia, begins mobilizing for war on July 29

August 1: Germany declares war on Russia

France is forced to mobilize in accordance with their agreement with Russia

August 3: Germany declares war on France, and German troops pour into neutral Belgium

British Foreign Secretary, Sir Edward Grey, sends an ultimatum to Germany to withdraw its troops from Belgium

August 4: Germany refuses to withdraw from Belgium

Britain declares war on Germany

August 23: Japan, in accordance with an alliance signed with Britain in 1902, declares war on Germany

August 4–September 6: Battle of the Frontiers

August 26–30: Battle of Tannenberg

September 6–10: First Battle of Marne

October 19: Start of the First Battle of Ypres

October 29: The Ottoman Empire (modern-day Turkey) enters the war on the side of the Central Powers and assists Germany in a naval bombardment of Russia

November 2:   Russia declares war on the Ottoman Empire

November 5: Britain and France declare war on the Ottoman Empire

November 22: End of the First Battle of Ypres

December 24–25: Christmas Truce on the Western Front

1915

February 19: Start of the naval bombardment of the Dardanelles

March 18: End of the naval bombardment of the Dardanelles

April 22: Start of the Second Battle of Ypres

April 25: Start of Gallipoli Campaign

May 7:   German U-Boat sinks the Lusitania

May 23: Italy joins the war on the side of the Allies

May 25: End of the Second Battle of Ypres

September 25: Start of the Battle of Loos

October 8: End of the Battle of Loos

1916

January 9: End of Gallipoli Campaign

February 21: Start of the Battle of Verdun

May 31–June 1: Battle of Jutland

> June 4: The Russian June Offensive, including the Brusilov Offensive, is launched on the Eastern Front to coincide with the Battle of the Somme

July 1: Start of the Battle of the Somme

September 20: End of the Russian Offensive

November 18: End of the Battle of the Somme

December 18: End of the Battle of Verdun

1917

March 15: Tsar Nicholas is forced to abdicate from the Russian throne, ending 304 years of Romanov rule

Tsar Nicholas is replaced by a provisional government

April 6: United States of America joins the war

July 1–19: Russian July Offensive (Kerensky Offensive) on the Eastern Front

November 6–7: Revolution breaks out in Russia, and the provisional government is overthrown by the Bolsheviks

1918

March 3: Russia signs the Treaty of Brest-Litovsk with the Central Powers, and war ends in Russia

July 17: Tsar Nicholas and his family are murdered at Yekaterinburg

August 8: Start of the Hundred Days Offensive

November 11: The First World War officially ends on the eleventh hour of the eleventh day of the eleventh month

Contents

Introduction

"Dulce et Decorum est"

By Wilfred Owen

Bent double, like old beggars under sacks,

Knock-kneed, coughing like hags, we cursed through sludge,

Till on the haunting flares we turned our backs,

And towards our distant rest began to trudge.

Men marched asleep. Many had lost their boots,

But limped on, blood-shod. All went lame; all blind;

Drunk with fatigue; deaf even to the hoots

Of gas-shells dropping softly behind.

Gas! GAS! Quick, boys!—An ecstasy of fumbling

Fitting the clumsy helmets just in time,

But someone still was yelling out and stumbling

And flound'ring like a man in fire or lime.—

Dim through the misty panes and thick green light,

As under a green sea, I saw him drowning.

In all my dreams before my helpless sight,

He plunges at me, guttering, choking, drowning.

If in some smothering dreams, you too could pace

Behind the wagon that we flung him in,

And watch the white eyes writhing in his face,

His hanging face, like a devil's sick of sin;

If you could hear, at every jolt, the blood

Come gargling from the froth-corrupted lungs,

Obscene as cancer, bitter as the cud

Of vile, incurable sores on innocent tongues,—

My friend, you would not tell with such high zest

To children ardent for some desperate glory,

The old Lie: *Dulce et decorum est*

Pro patria mori.

Since the Great War is no longer a part of living memory and none remain alive to talk of their experiences, the words of men like Wilfred Owen are becoming more and more significant. They are keeping the memory of the war alive and providing vital lessons for future generations. In those 28 lines, Owen brings to life the horror and suffering of the First World War. He encapsulates the significance of the war and how it not only ripped apart the lives of individuals but also the social fabric of the world, and destroyed long-held beliefs of honor and glory. For those returning from the front, and those who had remained on the home front, the world that they had once known and fought so hard to defend no longer existed after 1918.

The First World War was one of the most devastating conflicts in our history. The death toll was like nothing experienced before, and it is estimated that there were about 37 million civilian and military casualties, with deaths of about 10 million military personnel. Some were vaporized or blown apart by mortar shells and artillery fire, and others remain buried in some forgotten poppy-filled field of Europe. Regardless of how people remember the First World War, and whether or not they romanticize the life of a soldier on the front lines, it is important that the world never forgets this brutal and bloody conflict. At the Battle of the Somme, the British Army alone sustained 54,470 casualties with 19,240 deaths in a single day. That was the scale of the tragedy that engulfed the world from 1914 to 1918, and it played itself out primarily across Europe but also spilled over into Asia and Africa.

The Great War changed the face of Europe. At the start of 1914, the mighty Austro-Hungarian Empire was a force to be reckoned with, Russia was a vast and unwieldy monarchy ruled for 304 years by the Romanov Dynasty, the Ottoman Empire could still command a degree of respect, Britain was master of the seas, and Germany was the relatively new kid on the block, looking for an opportunity to flex her military muscles and cement a place in history.

Trench warfare became a hallmark of the war as troops on both sides got bogged down on the Western Front and resorted to a war of attrition, trying to wear each other down and reduce the enemy's effectiveness through a sustained and prolonged attack in an attempt to break the deadlock. The First World War was a war the likes of which the world had never seen, and this was partly due to the scale of the conflict but also because of changes in military technology and weapons. By the start of the 20th century, technology had dramatically changed the nature of warfare, but military commanders throughout the world had yet to grasp the true implications and impact of these changes on the battlefield and battle strategy. When war broke out, the armies on both sides expected to use entrenchments as cover from enemy fire and to seize positions from which to provide cover fire for the next phase of an attack. The military leaders never expected the armies to stay hunkered down and for the trenches to become the main feature of the conflict.

Military commanders had assumed that artillery attacks would be able to destroy the trenches or at least pin the troops down long enough to allow for an effective infantry or cavalry attack. This, however, was not the case, and on the Western Front the war was won and lost in the trenches. But victory came at a heavy cost as the Western Front soon became a stalemate with both sides suffering heavy casualties but gaining almost no ground. The Battle of Verdun, the longest and one of the bloodiest battles of the First World War, dragged on for almost a year with neither side making much headway. That was the unanticipated nature of trench warfare.

The war on the Eastern Front was far more fluid and mobile but no less brutal and horrific. Millions died on the front, not just from their wounds, but from cold, disease, and lack of supplies. Russia used its numerical advantage to push the Germans back time and again, but in the end, the devastating loss of life and suffering of the Russian people ended the rule of the Romanov Dynasty, sounded the death knell of the once mighty Russian Empire, and gave rise to communism.

The Gallipoli Campaign was an unmitigated disaster for the Allies, but it was the coming of age of the Anzac (Australian and New Zealand Army Corps) troops who demonstrated their tenacity and courage under enemy fire. But more than that, it was the making of Mustafa Kemal Atatürk, the man who would go on to become the father of modern Turkey.

At the conclusion of the First World War in November 1918, the world was a very different place than what it had been a mere four years earlier, and the borders of Europe were being redrawn. The Russian, Ottoman, and Austro-Hungarian Empires no longer existed, Germany was beaten into submission with the world believing it would not rise again, and France and Britain had come out on top.

But the tumult and chaos that remained in the wake of the First World War had far-reaching and devastating consequences, not just for Europe and the survivors of the war, but for the entire world. The ruins of Europe provided a fertile breeding ground for fierce nationalism, which led to the rise of the Third Reich and allowed the evil of Adolf Hitler to go unchecked for far too long.

Chapter One – The Fatal Shots That Set the Stage for War

June 28, 1914 is one of the most infamous days in world history. On that day, gunshots rang out on a street in Sarajevo and reverberated around the world. The assassination of Archduke Franz Ferdinand and his wife, Sophie, Duchess of Hohenberg, set off a chain reaction that triggered the First World War. But how had the world come to the point where an assassination of an unpopular royal could have such devastating and far-reaching consequences?

The issue of succession in the Austro-Hungarian Empire was complicated. When Emperor Franz Joseph's only son Rudolf committed suicide, Archduke Franz Ferdinand, the nephew of the emperor, became heir to both the Austro-Hungarian Empire and the Habsburg throne. Emperor Franz Joseph did not approve of his nephew or his marriage to Sophie Chotek von Chotkova. Franz Joseph considered Sophie to be inferior in rank and birth as she was not descended from any ruling European dynasty. He made his displeasure at their union obvious by not attending the wedding and excluding any of Franz Ferdinand and Sophie's offspring from the line of succession. Franz Joseph may not have been able to choose his own heir, but he was able to use his power to bar Franz Ferdinand and Sophie's children from inheriting the Austro-Hungarian throne.

Unfortunately, politics in Austro-Hungary at the time were just as complicated as the succession to the throne. There had been conflict in central Europe for centuries as the various countries, empires, and principalities vied for power. When Austria annexed Bosnia-Herzegovina in 1908, many Serbs were dissatisfied, and this led to continuous tension and clashes between the Serbs and the Austro-Hungarian Empire. It was this ongoing tension that ultimately led to the assassination of Franz Ferdinand and Sophie by a Bosnian Serb student named Gavrilo Princip.

Gavrilo Princip had devoted his life to protecting Serbia, and he saw the visit of Archduke Franz Ferdinand as the perfect opportunity to make a political statement. He enlisted the help of a small group of supporters and, with assistance from the Black Hand, a secret Serbian society founded in the early 20th century to promote the liberation of Serbs outside Serbia, he was able to acquire pistols, bombs, and poison for his group of fanatics to use to carry out their suicide mission.

Franz Ferdinand was in Sarajevo overseeing military maneuvers and inspecting troops in the newly annexed Bosnia-Herzegovina. It was his wedding anniversary, and therefore, the normally sidelined Sophie was traveling with him in an official capacity. As part of this royal visit, there were numerous ceremonies and celebrations that the archduke and his wife were attending throughout their stay. Unfortunately, the day they chose to be out and about inspecting troops was not an auspicious date as it was also the anniversary of the First Battle of Kosovo—the day in 1389 when Serbian independence was crushed by the Ottoman Empire.

On that fateful day, the royal couple traveled through Sarajevo in an open-topped car with minimal security. Princip and his band of would-be assassins had positioned themselves at various intervals along the motorcade route and waited for an opportunity to present itself. That they actually managed to carry out this assassination is something of a surprise. They were certainly not trained for this type of operation and seemed more like a hapless band of fanatics rather than successful assassins. Had their mission not had such devastating consequences, it could almost be viewed as a comedy of errors. One of the assassins couldn't get his bomb out of his pocket in time to throw it at the passing motorcade, and another managed to throw his bomb, but it bounced off the convertible roof of the car and exploded against the wheel of another vehicle, causing no significant damage or injuries. One assassin positioned himself too close to a policeman to attempt an attack, another had second thoughts, and the last member of the group ran away. And as for Princip? He was never in a position to take a shot and thought that they had missed their opportunity.

But luck or destiny turned out to be on Princip's side, and by a cruel twist of fate, their paths eventually did cross that day. After his official visits, Franz Ferdinand decided to go to the hospital to visit the men that had suffered minor injuries in the bomb attack. On the way to the hospital, there was some confusion between Franz Ferdinand and his driver, and when they stopped the vehicle in the road to decide on the best route, Princip just happened to find himself in the perfect position to assassinate his target. He was able to draw his pistol and shoot both Archduke Franz Ferdinand and Sophie at point-blank range. Both his shots found their mark, and within half an hour, the Archduke and his wife had succumbed to their wounds. Princip had planned the assassination as a suicide mission, so as soon as he had shot Franz Ferdinand and Sophie, he turned the pistol on himself, but the crowd prevented him from taking his own life. He then drank the poison that the Black Hand had provided but that only made him vomit. He was immediately arrested by the police, but as he was too young to receive the death penalty, he was sentenced for the maximum of twenty years in prison, where he would die due to tuberculosis..

One has to wonder if Princip would have continued with his ill-conceived plan if he had known that his act of patriotism would have such far-reaching and bloody consequences, or perhaps his feelings of nationalism were so strong that nothing would have stood in his way. Or would he have found validation in the fact that, by the end of the First World War, the Austro-Hungarian Empire had collapsed and a new world order had emerged? The answers to these questions will never be known, but the tragic consequences of what can be described as a coincidental, and almost unbelievable, chain of events remains. Instead of being a minor ripple in history, the assassination of the unpopular Archduke Franz Ferdinand was only the beginning of a horrific and bloody age, the consequences of which can still be felt today, more than 100 years after those fatal shots were fired.

On the face of it, nobody would have predicted that the assassination of Archduke Franz Ferdinand would be a world-changing event. While none of the world leaders were overly upset by Franz Ferdinand's untimely death, it did set off a chain of events that led to the mobilization of almost all the armies across Europe, including Austria-Hungary, Serbia, Russia, France, the Ottoman Empire, and Germany. At first glance, the fallout from the assassination seems extreme, but if one looks a little deeper, you will see that the Austro-Hungarian Empire was itching for a fight and just looking for any excuse to attack Serbia. By attempting to strike a blow for Serbia, Princip and his hapless band of assassins played right into their hands.

The Austrian government immediately blamed Serbia, their troublesome neighbor, for the assassination of their archduke. However, instead of immediately taking action, Austria-Hungary first ensured that they had the support of their most powerful neighbor, Germany, and only a month after the assassination, on July 28, 1914, did they declare war on Serbia. Serbia, recognizing the threat that Austro-Hungary posed to their independence, had not been sitting idle for a month; they too had been gathering support and preparing for conflict. By the time the Austro-Hungarian Empire declared war, Serbia had used a treaty they held with Russia to ensure that they had the support of this vast empire on their doorstep. When Serbia called on Russia for support, Russian then invoked its treaties with both France and Britain. This meant that by the time Austria-Hungary declared war on Serbia the conflict was no longer between two disgruntled neighbors. Within days of Austria declaring war on Serbia, events moved swiftly as various alliances came into play, governments began choosing sides, and countries mobilized for war.

The entire situation had snowballed out of control and put two major factions in Europe on a war footing. On one side there was Serbia and the Allies, namely France, Britain, and Russia, and on the other side, there was Germany and Austria-Hungary, known as the Central Powers. Numerous other countries joined the war later for various reasons, but regardless of what was to come, by July 28, 1914, war on a large scale in Europe was inevitable.

Timeline of Initial Countries Entering the War in 1914

July 28, 1914: The Austro-Hungarian Empire declares war on Serbia

Germany immediately allies itself with the Austro-Hungarian Empire and declares war on Serbia

Russia, in accordance with its alliance with Serbia, begins mobilizing for war on July 29

August 1: Germany declares war on Russia

France is forced to mobilize in accordance with their agreement with Russia

August 3: Germany declares war on France, and German troops pour into neutral Belgium

British Foreign Secretary, Sir Edward Grey, sends an ultimatum to Germany to withdraw its troops from Belgium

August 4: Germany refuses to withdraw from Belgium

Britain declares war on Germany

August 23: Japan, in accordance with an alliance signed with Britain in 1902, declares war on Germany

October 29: The Ottoman Empire (modern-day Turkey) enters the war on the side of the Central Powers and assists Germany in a naval bombardment of Russia

November 2: Russia declares war on the Ottoman Empire

November 5: Britain and France declare war on the Ottoman Empire

And so, the stage was set for one of the greatest conflicts the world has ever seen.

Chapter Two – The Western Front and the First Battle of Marne

When war broke out, Germany was quite literally stuck in the middle, forced to fight a war on two fronts. With Russia to the east and France to the west, Germany had no choice but to divide their firepower and send their troops and resources in two opposite directions, leaving them in a weakened position. But the Germans had prepared for just such an eventuality and working from the Schlieffen Plan,[1] which identified France as the greater threat, they mobilized their main force to the west and marched on Paris while sending a smaller force east.

The German military command recognized that the only way to be victorious was to act swiftly and knock France out of the war before turning their full attention to Russia. The German-French border, however, was too heavily fortified and well defended to deliver the blitz attack the Germans needed to neutralize France. To this end, the Schlieffen Plan called for an attack through neutral Belgium. The unintended, but quite possibly not unanticipated, consequence of this move was to bring England into the war.

As planned, the German advance through Belgium was swift and met with little resistance. The French did manage to challenge the Germans and slow them down at the Belgium border in the Battle of the Frontiers. This engagement was comprised of five battles, fought between the German 2nd, 3rd, 4th, 5th, 6th, and 7th Armies, the French

1st, 2nd, 3rd, 4th, and 5th Armies, and the British Expeditionary Force (BEF) at Lorraine, the Ardennes, Charleroi, and Mons, during the opening months of the war.

The French forces were quickly destroyed by the advancing Germans in Lorraine on August 20. This was followed by the bloody battles of Ardennes and Charleroi which were fought from August 21 to 23, where approximately 27,000 French soldiers died. On August 23, the British Expeditionary Force, who were supposed to support the French 5th Army, found themselves unable to assist their allies as they had to fight their own battle at Mons. To make matters worse, the roads were crowded with Belgian refugees, and soon the French Army was collapsing all along the line from Lorraine to the Meuse.

General Lanrezac, commander of the French 5th Army, realizing that his men were being pushed to their limits, ordered a general retreat. He believed retreat would be preferable to the total destruction of the 5th Army as, in his mind, this would be a catastrophe for France. He reportedly told one of his officers, "We have been beaten but the evil is reparable. As long as the 5th Army lives, France is not lost." The Battle of the Frontiers was a costly failure for France, and the total number of casualties was estimated to be 260,000 with 140,000 of them occurring on just the last four days alone, but the French 5th Army did survive to fight another day.

The Allies were unable to halt the German onslaught at their border, and the invading army broke through the French defenses and continued to march toward Paris. With the Germans steadily advancing, Paris now prepared itself for battle, and on September 2, the French government evacuated to Bordeaux, leaving General Gallieni in charge of the defense of the city. The German 1st and 2nd Armies were ordered to approach Paris as a unit, but the 1st Army, under the command of General von Kluck, chose instead to pursue the retreating French 5th Army. This turned out to be a bad move as it created a gap between the two German armies and exposed the

German 1st Army's right flank, making it susceptible to a French counterattack.

The French knew that if they came under direct attack, Paris would not be able to hold out for long against the Germans, and so when General Gallieni received word that Kluck was pursuing the French 5th Army, he urged his commanders to launch a surprise attack against the Germans before they could reach Paris. Fortunately, Gallieni had the support of French General Joseph Joffre, who was of the same mind and felt that the opportunity for a counterattack was too good to resist. This was a surprising and ambitious plan. To all intents and purposes, the German Army had the French on the run, and the troops on both sides were exhausted from the long, fast march south from the Belgium border. The French did, however, have the advantage of being closer to Paris and fresh supplies, while the German supply lines were getting longer and more stretched out.

On September 6, 1914, the First Battle of Marne began. The French 6th Army, under the command of General Michel Maunoury, attacked the German 1st Army that was moving south rapidly in pursuit of the French 5th Army. When they came under attack, the German 1st Army moved west to confront their attackers, increasing the gap between them and the main body of the German army. At first, it appeared that Gallieni's ambitious plan had failed and that the battle would go the way of the Germans. The French Army was on the verge of defeat when they received timely reinforcements from 6,000 soldiers of the 103rd and 104th regiments stationed in Paris.

What made the arrival of these troops at the Battle of Marne astonishing was their mode of transport. At first, there appeared to be no way to get the much-needed reinforcements to front lines in time to influence the outcome of the battle, but General Gallieni was an inspired man and used Parisian taxi cabs to ferry the troops to Marne. This was the first automotive transport of troops in any war in history, and the "Taxis of Marne" were Renault taxi cabs that police officers, under the orders of General Gallieni, requisitioned in the streets of Paris. The 630 taxi cabs played a vital role in keeping Paris from falling into enemy hands and illustrate the lengths to which the French were willing to go to protect their capital. The speedy arrival of the troops enabled the French and English to hold back the German Army, keep them out of Paris, and dash any hopes that the German army had of a swift victory on the Western Front.

While the French 6th Army was battling the German 1st Army, the French 5th Army, now under the command of General Louis Franchet d'Esperey, and British troops led by Field Marshal John French pushed forward into the gap between the divided German forces and attacked the 2nd Army. The Germans were caught entirely off guard by this proactive move from the French, and confusion amongst the ranks allowed the Allies to halt the German attack.

The Battle of Marne was a victory for the French as they succeeded in halting the German advance on Paris, but it was a hard fought and bloody affair. Casualties were estimated to be 250,000 on each side. Even though this battle was fought at the start of the war, it was a very significant event and one of the decisive battles of the First World War. By halting the German attack and pushing them back from Paris, the allies negated the Schlieffen Plan, ensuring that the war would continue for another four years. A war that many thought would be over by Christmas 1914 was now destined to continue, causing untold misery and ultimately playing a pivotal role in the rise of the Third Reich and the outbreak of the Second World War.

[1]*The Schlieffen Plan was drawn up in the early 20th century by Alfred Graf von Schlieffen, chief of the German Great General Staff from 1891 to 1905. The plan was developed to swiftly and effectively deal with a two-front war. The success of the Schlieffen Plan called for a swift military resolution on the Western Front so that Germany could then turn their full attention on Russia before the mighty Russian war machine had time to fully mobilize; this was predicated on the belief that it would take at least six weeks for the Russians to be in a position to attack Germany. This meant that, in the event of a two-front war, Germany would initially only need to place a nominal*

number of troops on the Eastern Front and could then use the bulk of their army and supplies to launch a swift attack through Belgium in the west. At the beginning of the 20ᵗʰ century, France had heavily fortified their border with Germany, and the Germans knew that a direct attack would take months. Therefore, Schlieffen advocated bypassing these fortifications and invading France via a fast march through neutral Belgium. Schlieffen was so confident in the strength of his plan that he calculated it would take a mere 42 days to complete, and when Germany was faced with a war on two fronts, they put the Schlieffen Plan into motion.

Chapter Three - War in the Trenches

Trench warfare, which has become synonymous with the First World War, began at the First Battle of Marne. At the beginning of the 20th century, technology had dramatically changed the nature of warfare, but the armed forces had yet to grasp the true implications of it. Military leaders expected to use entrenchments as cover and positions from which to launch an attack. They never anticipated that their armies would get bogged down in the trenches and that they would be facing a new type of land warfare that would quickly become the main hallmark of the conflict on the Western Front.

On September 9, 1914, the German advance on the Western Front had been halted by the French, and the Germans had retreated to the border of the Aisne River where they began regrouping. It was here, in one of his last acts as German Chief of the Great General Staff, that Helmuth von Moltke gave one of the most significant orders of the war. He ordered the German troops to begin digging the first trenches of the First World War. Even though this process took nearly two months to complete, it was still only meant to be a temporary measure against French retaliation. But in effect, von Moltke's order changed battlefield tactics forever—gone were the days of open warfare, as both sides hunkered down and remained in their trenches for the duration of the war on the Western Front.

Initially, the trenches were intended to be nothing more than temporary shelters and simple constructions designed to be packed with men fighting shoulder to shoulder, but as the war dragged on and everyone realized that trench warfare had become an integral part of the battle plan, the architecture of the trenches became more significant and elaborate. Before long, a maze of complex communications and supply trenches ran up to the front lines and connected to the battle trenches as both sides constructed an elaborate system of zigzagging frontline corridors, underground tunnels, traverses, firing recesses, and dugouts. The Anzac forces in Gallipoli went so far as to bring in engineers, who had honed their skills in gold mines, to help design and construct their trenches.

A well-designed trench was at least 8 feet (2.5 meters) deep so that men could walk upright and still be protected from enemy fire. The banked earth on the top of the trench facing the enemy was called the parapet and had a fire-step, where troops could stand to see out of the trenches and fire on the enemy. To see over the parapet, without being exposed to enemy fire, the troops used a trench periscope, often nothing more than a stick with two angled mirrors at the top and bottom. Some soldiers had periscope rifles that allowed the men to snipe at the enemy without exposing themselves to fire. The rear lip of the trench was called the parados and protected the soldiers' backs from shells falling behind the trenches. The floor of the trench was usually covered by wooden duckboards, and in later designs, the floor was raised on a wooden frame to provide for drainage. Trenches were further protected from assault by barbed wire, mines, netting, camouflaged pits, and other obstacles. Dugouts were constructed to be shell-proof and to resist both artillery bombardment and infantry assaults.

The ground separating the trenches of two opposing armies was known as no man's land. On the battlefield, this could be anything from 100 to 300 yards (90 to 275 meters), but it all depended on terrain and fighting conditions. On Vimy Ridge, the trenches were as close as 30 yards (25 meters), and on the narrow ridges near Chunuk Bair during the Gallipoli Campaign, the Anzac and Ottoman troops were separated by a mere 16 yards (15 meters), close enough to lob grenades and bombs into each other's trenches. Trench warfare was even seen in mountainous regions like the Alps, where trenches stretched deep into the mountains and up vertical slopes to heights of 12,800 feet(3,900 meters) above sea level.

Life in the trenches was unpleasant at best, but mostly it was downright horrendous. In Anzac Cove on the Gallipoli Peninsula, fighting was particularly intense with heavy casualties on both sides. In the summer heat, conditions in the trenches rapidly deteriorated and became appalling. Food spoiled quickly, illness was widespread, and large swarms of black corpse flies covered everything as the bodies of the soldiers killed in battle piled up in the trenches and ravines, remaining there for weeks, unburied and rotting.

On the Western Front, the war became a struggle between equally matched armies and quickly turned into a battle of attrition. As the continuous trenches had no open flanks that could be attacked, vast numbers of troops were sent over the top and were quickly cut down by artillery and machine-gun fire. It was often impossible to remove the bodies or rescue the wounded from no man's land, and thousands of injured soldiers were left lying in the hot sun or freezing mud for days, screaming in pain and pleading for water until they eventually died where they lay. Ultimately, the war was won by the side that was able to commit and sacrifice the greatest number of men on the Western Front.

British artist, Paul Nash, described his experience on the Western Front in a letter to his wife;

> I have just returned, last night, from a visit to Bde ([Brigade] HQ up the line, and I shall not forget it as long as I live. I have seen the most frightful nightmare of a country more conceived by Dante or Poe, unspeakable, utterly

indescribable...but only being in it and of it can ever make you sensible of its dreadful nature and what men in France have to face...Evil and the incarnate fiend alone can be master of the ceremonies in this war; no glimmer of God's hand is seen. Sunset and Sunrise are blasphemous, mockeries to man; only the black rain out of the bruised and swollen clouds on thro' the bitter black of night is fit atmosphere in such a land. The rain drives on; the stinking mud becomes more evilly yellow, the shell holes fill up with green white water, the roads and tracks are covered in inches of slime, the black dying trees ooze and sweat and the shells never cease. They whine and plunge over head, tearing away the rotting tree stumps, breaking the plank roads, striking down horses and mules; annihilating, maiming, maddening; they plunge into the grave which is this land; one huge grave, and cast up the poor dead. O it is unspeakable, Godless, hopeless. [1]

[1] Carroll, Andrew; *Behind the Lines, Revealing and Uncensored Letters from our War-Torn World,* p 117

Chapter Four – The Eastern Front and the Battle of Tannenberg

The First World War was fought on two fronts, the Western Front and the Eastern Front. Fighting on the Eastern Front stretched from the Black Sea in the south all the way to the Baltic Sea in the north. This was the dividing line between the Russian Empire and Romania on one side and the Austro-Hungarian Empire, Bulgaria, and Germany on the other. The battles fought on the Eastern Front were equally as bloody and devastating as anything experienced on the Western Front.

Unlike the Western Front, however, the war on the Eastern Front did not get bogged down in the trenches and remained a fluid and mobile war. The vast area covered by the Eastern Front meant that the terrain and fighting conditions varied considerably, but for the most part, they were horrendous and physically taxing. Where the terrain was relatively flat, large armies could move east and west with relative ease, and in the first five months, as the battle raged fiercely between Germany and Russia, the German troops on the Eastern Front marched from the border of Poland to the outskirts of Warsaw and back again twice. The Austro-Hungarian troops that invaded Serbia captured Belgrade only to be forced to retreat all the way back to the border again.

In the First World War, as with Napoleon's invasion of Russia some 100 years earlier, the region's weather, geography, and underdeveloped infrastructure played a crucial role in shaping the conflict on the Eastern Front. Harsh winters and long, inadequate supply lines have been the stumbling block of many an invading army in this region for centuries, and in the early stages of the First World War, it was no different. In Lithuania, however, troops had to contend with swampy marshes, dragging cannons and heavy artillery through the mud. In Poland, conditions weren't any better; first, the armies marched across the country in the heat and dust of late summer and then again in the pouring rain and mud of autumn and finally, and fatally for many, through the deep snow of winter.

The first significant battle on the Eastern Front, and one of the first big battles of the war, was the Battle of Tannenberg in August 1914 between the 206,000 strong Russian 2nd Army and the 170,000 troops of the German 8th Army. When Russia entered the war on the side of Serbia, dragging France along with them, Germany put the Schlieffen Plan into motion. As France immediately came under attack, Tsar Nicholas of Russia, who at the outbreak of the war commanded an army of approximately 1.3 million men, agreed to launch an offensive in East Prussia, a German province.

Within two weeks of war breaking out, the Russians were organizing a two-pronged attack against Germany and the Austro-Hungarian Empire. The plan called for the Russian 1st and 2nd Armies to advance on the outnumbered German 8th Army and crush them from two sides, the objective being to overrun East Prussia and draw German forces away from the Western Front. Since the Germans had sorely underestimated the time it would take for Russia to become a threat, the defense of the Eastern Front was left in the hands of the aging General Maximilian von Prittwitz and an army of approximately 170,000 soldiers. This also meant that the bulk of the German fighting machine was marching on Paris, and the Allies knew that it was crucial to open the war on the Eastern Front if they were to have any hope of victory.

The ambitious attack on East Prussia called for the 1st Army to advance from the east while the 2nd Army attacked from the south, effectively cutting off the German 8th Army from the rear. But even though Russia attacked within two weeks, Schlieffen had not been wrong in his estimations, and in their haste, the invasion of East Prussia took place before Russia was fully prepared for war. This attack in itself was not a bad strategy, and in fact, the battle plan was good, but the execution thereof, unfortunately, was not.

In order for the Russian campaign to succeed, it relied on a degree of mobility and agility that the Russian army just simply did not possess. The conception of the plan was solid, but it was brought down by the fundamental flaws of incompetent leadership, lack of preparation, and poor road and rail infrastructure. The last meaning that the Russians own doing became their undoing. Russia had deliberately left the roads and railways in Russian-occupied Poland in a poor state to provide a buffer between themselves and Germany and to ensure that a German attack would be severely hampered by a lack of transport infrastructure. Ultimately, this strategy worked against them, and it was the Russian supply lines that were hampered by the lack of reliable road and railway infrastructure. To make matters worse, the railway lines between the two territories also had to be redone because the gauge, or spacing of the lines, differed between Russia and Prussia. This was a laborious and time-consuming exercise that slowed down the vital Russian supply lines. In the First World War, reliable rail transport was critical to success on the battlefield, and no army was able to operate effectively once they advanced too far from their railheads.

On August 17, the Russian army crossed the eastern border of East Prussia, and the opening shots of the war on the Eastern Front were fired at the Battle of Stalluponen (present-day Lithuania). Here, the German I Corp, a division of the 8th Army under the command of General Hermann von Francois, faced off against the Russian 1st Army, under the command of General Rennenkampf. An aggressive frontal attack from Francois drove the Russians back toward their border, but General von Prittwitz, overall commander of the 8th Army, believed this strategy to be too dangerous as the Germans were seriously outnumbered. Consequently, he ordered Francois to call off his attack before he could capitalize on his unexpected victory. As the German troops withdrew to Gumbinnen, Rennenkampf resumed his slow advance into East Prussia. Von Prittwitz then launched an offensive against the Russian 1st Army on August 20. This time, the battle went in favor of the Russians, and they defeated 8 divisions of the German 8th Army. The Russian 2nd Army, led by General Samsonov, meanwhile was making steady headway in the southwest. But the two Russian Armies were still separated by the Masurian Lakes, and this proved to be a fatal flaw in their plan.

Successfully carrying out a two-pronged attack relies heavily on good communication and understanding between the commanders of the two armies, and this certainly did not exist in the Russian ranks. Samsonov and Rennenkampf, who disliked each other intensely, had a strained relationship, to put it mildly. They refused to meet or even speak to each other, and this lack of communication and coordination undermined any numerical advantage they possessed.

This lack of leadership and coordination was evident from the start of the campaign. While Rennenkampf beat back the 8th Army at Gumbinnen, Samsonov was under tremendous pressure to advance on Freidrich von Scholtz's XX Corps, leaving his troops exhausted and hungry, and their supply line in complete disarray. The Germans, however, were not faring much better at this point. General von Prittwitz, fearing that his forces would be attacked from the rear and cut off from their lines of retreat, met with his commanders, including General Paul Grunert, Lieutenant Colonel Max Hoffmann, General Georg Friedrich Wilhelm, and Graf von Waldersee, to discuss their strategy. Von Prittwitz wanted to retreat to behind the Vistula River, but Grunert and Hoffmann did not support this plan and suggested a counterattack instead. After much discussion, a decision was made to launch an assault against Samsonov's western flank.

At this point, a number of things happened that influenced the outcome of the battle. Firstly, General von Prittwitz was replaced by General Paul von Hindenburg as commander of the 8th Army. Secondly, the Russians were careless with their communications, and the Germans intercepted uncoded Russian messages, including one that indicated that Rennenkampf was in no hurry to advance. This gave Von Hindenburg's chief of staff, Erich Ludendorff, time to refine Hoffmann's plan and concentrate six divisions against Samsonov's left flank in place of the original three. He then also took a calculated risk, based partly on the fact that Rennenkampf was not ready to attack, and withdrew the rest of his troops from Gumbinnen and positioned them to attack Samsonov's right flank. Using trains to quickly and efficiently move their troops, the Germans were able to surround Samsonov's forces before he realized what was happening.

On August 26, Samsonov's forces were spread out along a 60-mile front as they advanced on the German 8th Army and that's when Ludendorff ordered his six divisions to attack from the left flank. The Russian forces were caught completely by surprise, and by nightfall on August 29, after three days of relentless battering by German artillery, the Russians were surrounded. Samsonov ordered a retreat, but the Russian escape was cut off by German troops, and soon the 2nd Army was in complete disarray. Thousands were slaughtered on the battlefield or surrendered and were taken prisoner. By the end of August 1914, the Germans had decimated the Russian 2nd Army, and in the face of overwhelming defeat, on August 30, Samsonov walked into a forest and committed suicide.

Once the Germans had dealt with the 2nd Army and received reinforcements from the Western Front, they turned their attention on Rennenkampf's slowly advancing 1st Army and drove them out of East Prussia. The first major battle on the Eastern Front was a resounding success for the vastly outnumbered German army and brought considerable prestige to von Hindenburg and Ludendorff, who would go on to form a fabled duo and successfully plan and execute many more military campaigns. But the victory for the Germans was as much due to the errors made by the Russian generals and inadequate logistical support as it was to the military strategy of von Hindenburg and Ludendorff.

The events that led to the Russian defeat at Tannenberg were set in motion long before a single shot was even fired on the battlefield. Russia is a vast country with a large population that could contribute many able-bodied men to the war effort, but at the start of the First World War, they had a cumbersome and unwieldy army that was greatly hindered by internal politics and poor planning.

An army is only as effective as its supply lines, and without reliable access to ammunition, food, and other essentials, even the most powerful fighting force can be bought to its knees. Keeping the vast Russian war machine moving took careful planning and logistical precision. When the Russian commander, General Yakov Zhilinsky, signed an agreement with France that committed to the deployment of eight hundred thousand Russian soldiers into the field within two weeks of mobilization, he played a pivotal role in Russia's defeat at the Battle of Tannenberg. Committing this number of troops in such a short time overwhelmed the lumbering Russian war machine that was not designed to move quickly. It put a strain on the entire military operation and meant that many command decisions were taken in haste and under pressure without all the necessary information to implement an otherwise well-conceived plan.

The Battle of Tannenberg was a crushing defeat for the Russians, and by the end of August 1914, their ambitious plan to invade East Prussia was in tatters. The 2nd Army was practically annihilated, the Russian Army sustained at least 120,000 casualties of whom 92,000 were taken prisoner, and a vast amount of military equipment had been sacrificed on the battlefield for almost nothing. To make matters worse, the Russian command was not prepared for the scale of the battle, and sadly no one had anticipated the vast number of casualties that would need to be treated on the battlefield and transported to hospitals. As a result, many of the wounded and dying were left suffering for days, or even weeks, with little to no medical attention.

The Battle of Tannenberg lasted four days, from August 26 to 30, 1914, and was a resounding success for the Germans, demonstrating that in modern warfare a smaller force could defeat a far larger army on the battlefield with sound military tactics. It demonstrated the importance of logistical support and secure communications and showed that, regardless of the size of the army, without competent leadership victory was impossible. War was no longer a numbers game, and the side with the most troops would not necessarily emerge victorious. Unfortunately for the Russians, this battle highlighted their declining military power and set the tone for their entire involvement in the First World War.

And it wasn't just on the battlefields of East Prussia that people suffered. No one had anticipated the scale of loss and destruction that the Great War would bring to Europe. On the Eastern Front, there were widespread civilian casualties as the Austro-Hungarian Empire attempted to crush Serbia. Their first invasion ended in a humiliating retreat, but in the second offensive, the Austro-Hungarian Army managed to capture Belgrade before once again being forced to retreat. The Serbs were ultimately triumphant, but victory came at a heavy price as much of Serbia was devastated by the constant fighting, and when winter set in, disease spread across the country, and tens of thousands of soldiers and civilians died.

The one and only bright spot for the Allies, from the otherwise grim outcome of the Battle of Tannenberg, was that the Germans were forced to divert some of their troops away from the battles being waged on the Western Front. The two corps that were sent to the Eastern Front did not arrive in time to play a role in the Battle of Tannenberg, but they were also not present at the Battle of Marne, and this made it easier for British and French forces to launch a counterattack and halt the German advance on Paris, resulting in a crucial victory for the Allies.

Chapter Five - The Battle of Ypres and the Christmas Truce

Once the French had beaten the Germans back at the Battle of Marne, the Race to the Sea began as both sides fought to gain control of Belgian outlets to the North Sea. The armies tried desperately to outflank each other and move northward, constructing trenches as they went. Eventually, the Race to the Sea culminated in the Battle of Ypres, outside the historic Flemish town situated on the northern coast of Belgium. Ypres was strategically important to the Allies because it provided a defensive position from which to protect French ports in the English Channel. It was equally as important to the Germans because if they could break through the Allied defenses and capture Ypres, and other channel ports, then they would control all access to the North Sea.

After the Germans had captured the Belgian city of Antwerp, the British Expeditionary Force (BEF) and Belgian troops withdrew to Ypres to reinforce the Belgian and French troops stationed there. On October 19, 1914, the Allied and German forces engaged in the first of three battles to gain control of this tactical position. The area between the two opposing armies, the British at Ypres and the Germans at Menin and Roulers, became known as the Ypres Salient. Here, 34 German divisions faced off against 12 French, 9 British, and 6 Belgian divisions. This was the start of a long and protracted campaign, and the fields of Flanders would see some of the bloodiest and most brutal battles of the war.

The Battle of Ypres can best be described as a war of attrition, with neither side gaining much ground for the cost in human life and suffering on the fields of Flanders. From October 21 to 23, the Allied field defenses repulsed the relentless German attacks at Langemarck, and the Germans lost up to 70% of their men for very little tactical gain. Neither side could move troops to Ypres fast enough to crush the other army and gain a decisive victory. By the start of November, all the armies were short of ammunition and supplies, and the men were exhausted, leading to low morale and in some instances even refusal by soldiers to follow orders. The heavy losses continued on both sides until the onset of the harsh winter weather bought fighting to a halt.

The conditions at Ypres were terrible, as later described by Corporal Edward Williams:

> *On the night of 31 October, we took rations up to the battalion – they weren't there! We waited for hours under shell fire and rain, without being able to deliver them. The battalion had been moved at the end of the day to take over the front line of shell holes in the front of the destroyed village of Hooge on the Menin Road. In that lunar landscape, they got off course because they only had compass bearings. So the brigade decided that the rations would go up in daylight. It had been drenching rain and we could hardly move. Luckily, the visibility was poor – it was very misty – otherwise we would've been shelled to hell! We passed bogged 18-pounder guns and corpses: hands sticking out of the mud, faces floating in the shell holes. We came out at the*

top of the rise, and there was a bit of old trench, in which there were two dead Germans – one lying on his face, the other leaning against a wall. He was a handsome bloke; he reminded me of my father a bit. A shell had dissected him nicely, It had taken off the whole of the front of his chest down to his stomach – neatly cut aside and laid apart as if he was in the anatomy school. I said: "What a fantastic exhibition of anatomy!" It sounds heartless but then you're in an area of suppressed emotion, so your mind tends to take over. In front of us was broken ground – shell hole after shell hole after shell hole. It was our battalion, and my brother up there with his Lewis gun. He told me later that he'd looked back and seen the mule train as shapes in the mist! Nothing could be as wicked as the Ypres Salient. The Somme was bad – the Somme was terrible – but the Ypres had a vicious look all of its own.[1]

The Battle of Ypres clearly demonstrated that war was changing, and battles between massive armies equipped with modern weapons often proved to be indecisive. With effective field fortifications and the defensive use of artillery, one army could effectively neutralize many of the enemy's offensive weapons. The ability of armies to use trains and trucks to resupply their front lines and move troops swiftly from one battlefield to the next meant that battles were rarely quick and decisive; instead, they often dragged on for weeks. By the end of 1914, much of the fighting on the Western Front had reached a stalemate, and there was a lull in the action as commanders on both sides reconsidered their options.

Christmas 1914 was a bleak and bitter one in Europe. There was little cheer in the cold and muddy trenches as the bodies of the fallen lay stiff and frozen in no man's land, neither side having had the opportunity to retrieve and bury their dead. The men bogged down in the trenches around Ypres and the rest of France and Belgium had little to look forward to, other than more misery and another year of fighting.

This was not at all what the world had envisioned when the battle lines were drawn in August 1914. When the first armies marched out to face each other on the Western and Eastern Fronts, many on both sides believed that the war would be over quickly and everyone would be home by Christmas, enjoying Yuletide cheer with their families around a warm fire. The Germans had imagined that by implementing their well-conceived Schlieffen Plan they would be able to swiftly neutralize the threat on the Western Front and then turn their full attention to defeating the Russians. But this was not to be, and by Christmas 1914, Europe was embroiled in a war, the likes of which had not been seen before, and this was merely the beginning. Years of misery still lay ahead for war-torn Europe.

But amongst all this horror and destruction, some semblance of humanity still remained, and a certain degree of kinship was felt between the soldiers on both sides, leading to the emergence of some beautiful and inspiring stories from this time of widespread misery. One of the most enduring and much-loved stories of the First World War is the Christmas truce of 1914. On Christmas Eve, the guns had fallen silent, and in the eerie darkness, across the muddy expanse of no man's land, the British heard the Germans singing, "Stille Nacht. Heilige Nacht. Alles schläft, Eynsam wacht," the opening lines of "Silent Night." For many, this was probably the most beautiful sound they had heard in a long time. As the song came to an end, the British soldiers cheered and then responded by singing "The First Noel." The singing of hymns, carols, and folk songs back and forth across enemy lines continued throughout the night along the Western Front, and Christmas morning saw the soldiers leave their trenches to exchange Christmas greetings and, in some instances, souvenirs and food.

The Christmas truce was not an official ceasefire ordered by the high command on either side. It was rather a momentary, unilateral ceasefire instigated by the soldiers in the trenches, both before and on Christmas Day. It was a series of widespread and unofficial breaks in fighting along the Western Front, which gave troops a brief respite from battle and an opportunity to celebrate Christmas. During this ceasefire, there were also joint burial ceremonies, prisoner swaps, and the men even played games of football with one another. For many, this break in fighting probably seemed like the most beautiful Christmas gift they could have received amidst the horrors of war.

This situation came about in part because in December 1914 there was a brief lull in fighting as both sides took time to consider their options. The war had not gone according to plan for either side, and no one had anticipated a long-drawn-out fight. But that appeared to be exactly what they were now facing as a stalemate had developed between the Allies and the Central Powers following the indecisive result of the First Battle of Ypres.

The Christmas truce was unfortunately never repeated on the same scale as in 1914. In 1915, a few units organized ceasefires, but it was not widespread. This was partly due to orders from the commanders on both sides, but also the soldiers were no longer as amenable toward each other as they had been in 1914. As the war dragged and the fighting intensified, the men in the trenches became more bitter and disillusioned. After the devastation of Verdun and the Somme, attitudes toward the enemy hardened on both sides of the battle lines.

The poignant story of the Christmas truce clearly illustrates the human element of the war. Even now, more than 100 years later, it reminds people that the soldiers on both sides were just men and boys fighting for king and country, honor and glory, and to protect a way of life that they believed in. This war was not good versus evil and, regardless of how history has ultimately portrayed each side, in essence, these were just men doing their duty.

[1] Hart, Peter; "Mud, Blood and Gas" (BBC History Magazine, July 2017, p 47)

Chapter Six - Second Battle of Ypres and the Introduction of Chemical Warfare

The First World War introduced the age of chemical warfare to Europe. And no one can describe the effects of chlorine gas better than those who experienced it at the Second Battle of Ypres and bore witness to the horrific event that ushered in a new and frightening age of warfare.

Finally, we decided to release the gas. The weatherman was right. It was a beautiful day, the sun was shining. Where there was grass, it was blazing green. We should have been going on a picnic, not doing what we were going to do...We sent the infantry back and opened the valves with strings. After supper time, the gas started toward the French; everything was stone quiet. We all wondered what was going to happen. As this great cloud of green grey gas was forming in front of us, we suddenly heard the French yelling. In less than a minute they started with the most rifle and machine gun fire that I had ever heard. Every field artillery gun, every machine gun, every rifle that the French had, must have been firing. I had never heard such a noise. The hail of bullets going over our heads was unbelievable, but it was not stopping the gas. The wind kept moving the gas towards the French lines. We heard the cows bawling, and the horses screaming. The French kept on shooting. They couldn't possibly see what they were shooting at. In about 15 minutes the gun fire started to quit. After a half hour, only occasional shots. Then everything was quiet again. In a while it had cleared and we walked past the empty gas bottles. What we saw was total death. Nothing was alive. All of the animals had come out of their holes to die. Dead rabbits, moles, and rats and mice were everywhere. The smell of the gas was still in the air. It hung on the few bushes which were left. When we got to the French lines the trenches were empty but in a half mile the bodies of French soldiers were everywhere. It was unbelievable. Then we saw there were some English. You could see where men had clawed at their faces, and throats, trying to get breath. Some had shot themselves. The horses, still in the stables, cows, chickens, everything, all were dead. Everything, even the insects were dead.[1]

-Willi Siebert, German soldier recorded the first chlorine gas attack at Ypres

In 1915, the Germans were literally stuck in the middle of a war that was dragging on far longer than anyone had anticipated. They were bogged down in the trenches on the Western Front and facing off against the large Russian war machine on the Eastern Front. To distract the Allies from their impending spring offensive on the Eastern Front, the Germans launched a second, albeit limited, attack on Ypres. What made this battle significant was the insidious nature of the attack. Made up of four battles in the northern section of the Ypres Salient, the offensive was designed to probe the Allied defenses, but more importantly, it was an opportunity for the Germans to test their latest weapon on the Western Front—chlorine gas.

The plan was that the gas would be driven across no man's land by the wind and settle in the trenches. The panic-stricken French troops would be forced to retreat in order to avoid the choking fumes, thereby opening up a wide gap for the German soldiers, wearing gas masks, to push through and finally break the deadlock, taking control of the Ypres Salient. In order for the gas attack to work effectively, the Germans had to wait for the correct weather conditions so that the gas could be dispersed by the wind, and on April 22, 1915, the opportunity presented itself.

After some heavy artillery shelling, at 5 p.m. a greenish-yellow fog, several kilometers long, drifted across no man's land, carried on a gentle breeze, toward the French 45th Division trenches on the north side of the Ypres Salient, creating an eerie atmosphere. The soldiers on the Western Front had never seen anything like it before, and they did not recognize the fog as chlorine gas discharged by the Germans from pressurized cylinders along a fifteen mile stretch of the front line. As the gas, which is heavier than air, filled the trenches, the Allied troops began choking, spluttering, and struggling for breath. Those who were unable to escape died a horrific and painful death, clawing at their faces and scratching at their throats as the gas burned their skin and lungs.

Those who didn't succumb to the gas fled the trenches as their comrades flailed around, fighting for their lives, not against guns and bombs but against an even more frightening and insidious weapon. The gas attack, combined with the French retreat, tore a huge hole in the Allied defenses and threatened their position in the Ypres Salient, but the Germans failed to capitalize on their advantage. This was partly because they had underestimated the psychological impact of chemical warfare. The German troops, even wearing gas masks, were reluctant to advance through the gas, and soon the gaps that had been opened up by the attack were plugged by British and Canadian troops.

The Second Battle of Ypres was the Canadian Army's first major engagement in the war. Fortunately for them, they were not in the direct path of the first gas attack, but the French retreat exposed the Canadian left flank, and they were forced to shift position to cover the gap. For the following few days, the Canadians, outflanked, outgunned, and outnumbered, had to fight tooth and nail to defend their position and prevent the Germans from capitalizing on the effects of the gas attack. The Canadian counterattack stalled the German advance and bought the Allies the precious time they needed to move British troops forward and bolster the defense of the Ypres Salient. Their fierce fighting earned the Canadians a reputation for being tough and dependable.

Over the following four weeks, the British and Canadian units suffered heavy casualties as the Germans continued to attack the Allied trenches with artillery and gas, but the Allied defenses at Ypres Salient held firm, and on May 25, the Second Battle of Ypres ended. The battle was viewed as an Allied victory, but the initial chlorine gas attack led to almost 6,000 French casualties, as well as some unintended German casualties from exposure to their own deadly weapon.

The Second Battle of Ypres was not the first time that poison gas was used in the war. The Germans' first extensive use of poison gas was at the Battle of Bolimov on the Eastern Front, west of Warsaw, on January 31, 1915. At the time, the Germans were experimenting with this new form of warfare, and they fired 18,000 gas shells at the Russians without success. German General Max Hoffmann observed the gas attack from the top of a church in Bolimov, but the results were disappointing.

General Hoffmann had expected to witness the first successful chemical attack in Europe, but the gas, xylyl bromide, failed to vaporize in the freezing temperature and was blown back toward the German lines, falling harmlessly to the ground. When their gas attack failed, the Germans called off their assault on the Russian lines at Bolimov. The Russians launched a number of heavy counterattacks, but these were easily repulsed by the Germans, and little was achieved by either side.

The Russians were aware that the Germans had attempted an innovative use of poison gas, but because it had failed so spectacularly, the Russians basically ignored the threat and did not report it to the Allies on the Western Front. Unfortunately, the failure at Bolimov was only a temporary setback for the Germans. When chlorine gas was used in the more favorable conditions of the Western Front, it had the devastating effect that the Germans had hoped for. From then on, chemical attacks became a regular and horrifying feature of trench warfare and terrified soldiers more than any traditional weapon used against them. The consequences, however, were far more widespread and devastating than the casualties they caused on the battlefield.

[1] Everts, Sarah, "First-hand Accounts of the First Chlorine Gas Attack," https://chemicalweapons.cenmag.org/first-hand-accounts-of-the-first-chlorine-gas-attack/

Chapter Seven - Chemical Warfare on the Western Front

In a war of attrition, troop morale and mental stability are extremely important, and chemical agents are an insidious weapon that undermines both the mental and physical health of the men on the battlefield. In the First World War, far more soldiers were killed or injured by artillery attacks and gunfire than gas. Of the millions of casualties, only approximately 185,000 British service personnel were classified as gas casualties, and most of those were in the last two years of the war when mustard gas was introduced to the battlefield. The majority of men exposed to gas attacks went on to recover at least physically, but the psychological effects were far more damaging. And even when chemical gas attacks did not kill, they removed men from the battlefield for six to eight weeks, using up valuable medical resources and occupying much-needed beds. The gas also gave the trenches an eerie feeling; it was like a mist moving across the landscape, and the men with their gas masks looked like terrifying ghostly images. This horror was perfectly described in Wilfred Owen's "Dulce et Decorum Est."

Chlorine is the 17th element on the periodic table and has many industrial and practical applications, most notably forming the basis of household bleaches. When a small amount of chlorine is added to water, it forms hypochlorous acid that kills bacteria and prevents the growth of algae, making it an ideal pool cleaner. Used in these forms and in small quantities, chlorine is safe and non-lethal. But chlorine can be put to a much darker use, and that was clearly demonstrated during the First World War.

The possibility of chemical warfare was not a new concept at the start of the Great War. In 1899, a treaty had been signed by the European powers prohibiting the use of gas projectiles in battle. This treaty, however, did not stop the French launching shells containing a primitive form of non-lethal tear gas at the German lines in 1914 to disrupt the troops. The use of chlorine gas, however, was a whole different ballgame as it was specifically designed to kill. Incidentally, the pioneer of chemical warfare in Germany, Fritz Haber, planned to release the gas using canisters, not projectiles, and thereby staying within the letter of the 1899 treaty, if not the spirit. Many of the German officers were opposed to the use of chemical agents on the front lines, but Haber convinced them that the use of chlorine gas would significantly shorten the war and as a result save countless lives, and that the ultimate gains would be worth the casualties. When the German soldiers opened the valves of those first canisters on the Western Front, they had no idea what they were unleashing on the world.

Although the Allies condemned the use of chlorine gas at Ypres, they soon developed their own methods of dispersal, and within four months, at the Battle of Loos, the British attacked the German trenches with gas. Their officers used the excuse that their hand had been forced when the Germans had introduced chemical agents onto the battlefield, and they had no choice but to fight fire with fire if they hoped to win the war.

Commanders on both sides condemned the use of chemical weapons. General Karl von Einem, commander of the German 3rd Army, wrote, "I fear it will produce a tremendous scandal in the world...war has nothing to do with chivalry anymore." British Lieutenant General Charles Ferguson called it a cowardly form of warfare.

Haber had created a horrific weapon, and soon both sides were locked in a race to develop even more lethal and toxic chemicals to unleash on their enemies. There were three main types of chemicals developed and used by both sides on the battlefields of the First World War. Chlorine, with its familiar smell of bleach, reacts with fats, proteins, and other body fluids to attack the body in a number of ways and produce devastating internal and external chemical burns, with the gas corroding the eyes, mouth, nose, and lungs. Exposure to a small amount is not fatal, but there is no antidote, and high doses will either lead to a quick and merciful death or one that is excruciatingly slow and painful. In high doses, chlorine gas literally kills by asphyxiation as the chlorine reacts with moisture in the airways, forming hydrochloric acid and causing the lung tissue to swell and the victim to choke to death as they desperately fight for breath.

Other than chlorine gas, phosgene and mustard gas were also released in the trenches. Phosgene, which smells like moldy hay, is six times deadlier than chlorine gas and a much stealthier weapon. Phosgene was primarily used by the Allies and was responsible for 85% of chemical-related deaths in World War One. Soldiers did not know when they had been exposed to phosgene, much less received a fatal dose, and only after a day or so would their lungs fill with fluid and they would begin to slowly suffocate to death.

Mustard gas was the chemical agent most widely used in the First World War. This potent blistering agent, like phosgene, was not immediately detectable, and the effects were only felt hours after exposure. It did, however, have a potent smell that could be described as reeking of garlic, gasoline, rubber, or dead horses. Exposure in large quantities, without a gas mask, resulted in blisters in the lungs and throat and bloodshot eyes that became increasingly painful, in some instances even causing temporary blindness. The effects on soldiers wearing gas masks were equally as appalling. The mustard gas soaked through their woolen uniforms and blistered their skin, especially in the armpits and groin area. Contaminated uniforms need to be stripped off as quickly as possible and washed, but this was hardly practical for soldiers under attack on the front line. Later, as the blisters popped, they could easily become infected. The casualties from exposure to mustard gas were over 120,000 soldiers, but the death toll would have been much worse if the open air of the battlefield hadn't kept concentrations below the lethal threshold.

The true power of chemical warfare lay in their ability to not just kill and maim but also cause serious psychological damage, and the soldiers on the front lines were terrified of gas attacks. Many had watched their comrades choking and struggling for breath, so when the gas alert sounded, it caused widespread fear and panic amongst the men in the trenches. According to Professor Edgar Jones of King's Centre for Military Health Research in London, the fear of gas spread like a virus, and doctors on the front had to deal with scores of soldiers who thought they had been exposed to gas but displayed no symptoms. They were usually treated with a placebo, but this was an unproductive use of limited medical staff and resources, all adding to the pressures of fighting on the Western Front. Canadian soldiers urinated on cloths and used them to cover their faces during chlorine gas attacks. The ammonia in urine helps counteract the effects of the chlorine gas.

The Germans truly unleashed a monster on the world when they opened those first gas canisters at the Battle of Ypres, and contrary to Haber's prediction, the use of chemical weapons did nothing to shorten the war.

[1] Hart, Peter; "Mud, Blood and Gas" (BBC History Magazine, July 2017, p 47)

Timeline of Chemical Gas Attacks in the First World War

August 1914: French deploy tear gas grenades to disrupt German troops in the trenches.

October 1914: Germans fire 3,000 dianisidine chlorosulfate shells at the British Army at Neuve-Chapelle. The attack is ineffective because the chemicals were incinerated by the exploding shells.

January 1915: Germans fire 18,000 shells filled with xylyl bromide at the Russians at the Battle of Bolimov. The shells are ineffective as the cold keeps the liquid from vaporizing.

April 1915: Germany launches the first large-scale chemical attack at the Second Battle of Ypres. 5,730 cylinders of chlorine gas are released, and more than 1,000 French soldiers are killed and 7,000 injured.

September 1915: The British release chlorine gas from cylinders for the first time against the Germans at the Battle of Loos.

December 1915: The Germans use phosgene against the Allies killing 120 and injuring over 1,000.

July 1917: Mustard gas is used by the German for the first time and inflicts 2,100 casualties.

June 1918: The Allies begin using mustard gas against the Germans.

October 1918: Adolf Hitler is temporarily blinded by a gas attack near Ypres. He is evacuated to a military hospital and spends the remainder of the war recuperating.

November 1918 By the end of the First World War, there had been more than one million casualties caused by chemical weapons, including approximately 100,000 fatalities, primarily from phosgene poisoning.

1925: The Geneva Protocol, banning the use of chemical and biological warfare, is adopted by the League of Nations.

Chapter Eight - My Boy Jack, the Very Human Cost of the First World War

Millions of men died on the battlefields of the First World War. Bodies lay for days strewn across no man's land, and fields that were once green and fertile became nothing more than muddy quagmires of death and destruction. Men were buried where they fell in unmarked and unrecorded graves, interned forever far from home. In the immortal words of the poet Rupert Brooke, in one of his most famous poems, "The Soldier," "there's some corner of a foreign field that is forever England."

But the cost was not just in loss of life but also in unprecedented human suffering. Broken men were sent back from the front with horrific wounds, missing limbs, faces disfigured by shrapnel, and lungs destroyed by poison gas. These were the walking wounded. And those were just the visible wounds. Many more suffered from scars the world could not see; nightmares and shellshock (now known as PTSD) were widespread, and many never recovered, physically or psychologically, from what they had witnessed on the front. The once strong, able-bodied youth of Europe had been reduced to shuffling, bent over figures, old before their time. For them, there was no glory in war.

The families on the home front suffered just as much; they sacrificed husbands, sons, brothers, uncles, and heirs to the devastation that swept across Europe. There are a million different stories of loss and suffering, and it is hard to single out just one, but the story of Rudyard Kipling and his son, John, clearly demonstrates the very human cost of war. This was not just suffering on a grand scale; this was the very personal shadow of death that loomed over every family in Europe and many other parts of the world.

Rudyard Kipling was probably the most famous author of his age, the youngest Nobel literary laureate, and the voice of the empire, but the Great War spared no one. No family, regardless of fame or fortune, could escape the loss and heartbreak. For Rudyard Kipling, it was the carnage of the Battle of Loos in September 1915 which finally bought the war to his doorstep and plunged his life into darkness. His only son, John, was killed in action a mere six weeks after his 18th birthday, and like so many who died alongside him, this was John's first taste of war. Rudyard Kipling's loss was most likely compounded by the fact that he had pulled strings and used his connections and friendship with Lord Roberts, commander-in-chief of the British Army, to get John into the Irish Guards.

Even though John was declared dead soon after the battle, a witness having last seen him "stumbling blindly through the mud, screaming in agony after an exploding shell had ripped half this face apart," his remains were not found, and without a body, Kipling clung to hope and became obsessed with the idea that his son may have survived. Eventually, however, in 1919, after countless interviews with John's comrades and those who fought at Loos, Kipling had to accept that John was one of the 1.1 million British soldiers killed in the war.

Kipling may have publically acknowledged that his son had died at Loos, but he never wrote directly about John. The closest he came is

"My Boy Jack," a poem about a sailor that deals with loss, mourning, and regret. After the war, Kipling became a prominent member of the Commonwealth War Graves Commission and was instrumental in the creation of the stone graveyards to honor the fallen. He selected the epitaph, "Their Name Liveth For Evermore." Later, in "Epitaphs of the War," he wrote, "If any question why we died, Tell them, because our fathers lied." The death of his son at Loos shook Rudyard Kipling's belief in the British military command and more specifically in General Haig.

The Battle of Loos took place from September 25 to October 8, 1915. This was the biggest British attack of that year and the first time they used poison gas in the war. In an attempt to deliver a long-awaited breakthrough, the French focused their efforts on the heights of Vimy Ridge, while the British were expected to advance into the coal basin below. Apparently, without consideration for loss of life and despite the fact that his men were exhausted and his artillery had an insufficient supply of shells, British General Douglas Haig sent six divisions into the fray.

The southern end of the attack was successful on the first day, enabling the British, under the command of General French, to take the village of Loos and Hill 70 and then advance toward Lens. Unfortunately, their progress then ground to a halt due to the late arrival of reinforcements and a lack of munitions, allowing the Germans to counterattack and recapture Hill 70.

To the north, the British advance was slowed by the Hohenzollern Redoubt, a formidable and vast complex of German trenches, underground shelters, and machine gun nests. The machine gun nests proved to be particularly deadly for the British, with 8,500 men mowed down in a single day. For four days, the British bombarded the Germans with over 250,000 shells, but this had little effect. On the morning of September 25, knowing that he had insufficient artillery shells and to compensate for the ineffectiveness of the bombardment, General Haig ordered his officers to release 5,000 canisters of chlorine gas along the front line. The aim was to annihilate the Germans at Loos, and initially, the gas caused the desired panic amongst the Germans as approximately 600 men died in agony. However, the wind direction changed at several points along the front and blew the gas back into the Allied trenches, and 2,600 British troops had to be withdrawn from the battle.

On September 26, German reinforcements arrived to fill the breaches. But this did not stop 75,000 men going over the top of the trenches when the order came for them to attack, and the next British attack, launched without preliminary bombardments, resulted in a catastrophic loss of life as thousands of men were slaughtered by German machine gunners. After this, sporadic fighting continued until October 8 when the British commanders accepted the seriousness of the situation and ordered a retreat. On October 13, the British once again tried a gas attack, but this too came to a disastrous end when 180 officers and over 3,500 men of the 46th Division were killed in an attempt to take the Hohenzollern Redoubt. The failure at Loos led to General French being replaced as commander-in-chief by General Douglas Haig on December 19, 1915. Unfortunately, many of the mistakes made at Loos were repeated at the beginning of the Battle of the Somme.

Chapter Nine – The Gallipoli Campaign

By 1915, the British and the French were bogged down on the Western Front, the Russians were fighting a war of attrition on the Eastern Front, and nobody seemed to be making any headway. The Allied Powers then turned their focus on the Ottoman Empire, who had entered the war on the side of the Central Powers in November 1914, and more specifically Gallipoli, the narrow peninsula squeezed between the Aegean Sea and the Dardanelles in modern-day western Turkey. The Allies hoped to quickly seize control of the sea route from Europe to Russia by opening up the well-defended Dardanelles Strait, a narrow sea passage between the Aegean Sea and the Sea of Marmara.

Conceived by the First Lord of the Admiralty, Winston Churchill, the plan was a lightning strike designed to knock the Ottomans out of the war. Churchill saw the campaign as the Allies best hope of breaking the deadlock on the Western Front, and his generals expected the operation to be over in a matter of days. They calculated that an army of 50,000 men and overwhelming sea power would be all that was needed to knock the Ottoman Empire out of the war. To this end, in 1915, the Allies launched a naval assault to seize the Dardanelles Strait.

The assault on the Dardanelles began in mid-February with a long-range bombardment by British and French battleships. The repeated bombardment by the Allies, however, proved ineffective, and a month later, eighteen Allied battleships entered the strait in an attempt to force a passage up the Dardanelles. This attack did not go well for the Allies and resulted in three Allied battleships being sunk and a further three being badly damaged by Turkish fire and undetected mines.

In the wake of the failed naval assault, preparations began for a large-scale land attack on the Gallipoli Peninsula. What followed was the Battle of Gallipoli, or Dardanelles Campaign, that lasted from April to December 1915. British War Secretary Lord Kitchener appointed General Ian Hamilton to take command of the operation and lead a combined force, including French, British, and Anzac (Australian and New Zealand Army Corps) troops. The Allied troops gathered on the Greek island of Lemnos and prepared to launch their assault. At the same time as the Allies were preparing for the attack on the Gallipoli Peninsula, the Turks, under the command of the German General Liman von Sanders, were bolstering their defenses and positioning troops along the shore where they expected the landings to take place.

On the night of April 24, 1915, 32 Allied troop ships left Lemnos and advanced stealthily toward the Gallipoli Peninsula. This was the first amphibious assault in modern history, but unfortunately for the Allies, it was one of their greatest failures in the First World War. As the sun rose on April 25, 1915, the men on the boats could see the beaches of Gallipoli, heavily fortified with barbed wire, and the rugged limestone cliffs that lay just beyond them. The place looked deserted. But as the 1st Battalion of the Lancashire were preparing to land, they came under fire from the Ottoman troops on the higher ground, and as a hail of bullets rained down on them, chaos ensued. Trying desperately to escape the deadly attack, many soldiers leaped out of the boats and, weighed down by 70 pounds of kit, drowned in the deep water. Some, however, did manage to reach the beaches, only to be cut down by enemy fire as they got tangled up in the barbed wire. The few survivors of the Lancashire Fusiliers battalion pushed on and eventually forced the Turkish defenders to retreat. By 7:15 a.m., the Allies had secured the landing, but of the 1,029 men who had landed on the beach, only 410 survived.

Despite suffering these heavy losses, the Allies were able to secure two beachheads: The British 29th Division landed at Cape Helles and the Anzacs just north of the Gaba Tepe, later renamed Anzac Cove, on the Aegean coast. Both landings were met with stiff opposition from the Turks, and neither the British nor the Anzacs made any real forward progress. Soon the troops at Gallipoli were forced to hunker down, and in what was fast becoming an all-too-familiar scenario of the First World War, the Dardanelles campaign was fought from the trenches.

This is how Harold Elliot, Commander of the 7th Australian Battalion, described the conditions at Gallipoli and the bloody Battle of Lone Pine.

The Divisional Commander himself came down ...He saw with his own eyes the trenches choked with the dead and dying trodden on by their comrades because they could not be removed from the narrow trenches, and torn to pieces by the bombs and shells the enemy were hurling over... When anyone speaks to you of the glory of war, picture to yourself a narrow line of trenches two and sometimes three deep with bodies ... mangled and torn beyond description by the bomb and bloated and blackened by decay and crawling with maggots... we dug a huge tunnel back towards our own lines underground and packed in corpses in hundreds until it was full... [1]

In an attempt to break the deadlock on the peninsula and make some headway, the Allies launched a new assault in August and attacked the hills around Chunuk Bair, north of Anzac Cove. At the same time, they made another major troop landing at Sulva Bay. But this attack quickly stalled, largely due to Allied indecision and delay, allowing Ottoman reinforcements to arrive from both Palestine and the Caucasus, and once again a stalemate ensued. As Allied casualties mounted, General Ian Hamilton petitioned War Secretary Kitchener for 95,000 reinforcements but was offered barely 20,000.

By mid-October, the Allies had made little headway and suffered heavy casualties. General Hamilton estimated that a retreat would result in up to 50% loss of life. He was replaced by Sir Charles Munro, who recommended that the remaining 105,000 Allied troops be withdrawn from the peninsula as they were making no progress and conditions were appalling, the heat was suffocating, and the troops were surrounded by rotting corpses and thick swarms of corpse flies. In addition to this, they lacked fresh water, and thousands were dying from dysentery. On his recommendation, the government authorized the withdrawal of all Allied troops from Gallipoli. On December 7, 1915, the evacuation began from Sulva Bay and on January 9, 1916, the last troops left from Helles. At the end of the Gallipoli Campaign, 58,000 Allied soldiers and 87,000 Turkish soldiers had lost their lives, and approximately 300,000 had been seriously wounded, with the Allies having achieved nothing.

Allied success had depended on the Ottoman Turks being defeated quickly, but unfortunately, the Allies badly underestimated the strength of Turkish opposition and paid dearly for their mistake. The Ottoman Turks fought with discipline and tenacity that the British had never anticipated. They were also well dug in by the time the Allies landed and held the heavily fortified higher ground. Had this campaign, however, achieved its goal of securing the peninsula and allowing Allied ships to pass through the Dardanelles to capture Constantinople (modern-day Istanbul), it would have been a heavy blow to the Central Powers and may even have shortened the duration of the war. But unfortunately, this was not to be.

The fallout from the failure at Gallipoli led to the dramatic resignation of Britain's First Sea Lord Admiral John Fischer over the mishandling of the campaign by the First Lord of the Admiralty Winston Churchill. Later, Winston Churchill also resigned his post and accepted a commission to command an infantry battalion in France. The disaster of the Dardanelles hastened Asquith's resignation as prime minister of Britain, and he was replaced by David Lloyd George who would ultimately lead Britain to peace and play a pivotal role in drawing up the Treaty of Versailles.

Despite the Allied loss, the Gallipoli Campaign was one of the defining moments of the war and had a far greater influence on world history than anyone could have ever anticipated. It was a coming of age for the Australian and New Zealand (Anzac) troops as it demonstrated their courage and tenacity in a campaign that was doomed to fail from the start due to insufficient intelligence, lack of knowledge of the terrain, and unforeseen fierce Turkish resistance. For the Ottomans, it was a brief respite in the decline of their empire. But probably the most significant and enduring legacy of the campaign was that the victory was the making of a man named Mustafa Kemal.[2] This 33-year-old lieutenant colonel in the Ottoman army, who commanded the 19th Turkish Division, went on to become famous as Atatürk, the founder of modern Turkey.

[1] Carroll, Andrew; *Behind the Lines, Revealing and Uncensored Letters from our War-Torn World*, p 120 - 123

[2] *Atatürk was the founder and first president of the modern-day Republic of Turkey. Mustafa Kemal, born in 1881, in what was then still the Ottoman Empire, was raised to be a soldier and his father sent him to military school at the age of 12. From there, he progressed to the military academy in Constantinople, modern-day Istanbul. He graduated in 1905 and went straight into military service. He fought against the Italians in Libya and in the Balkan Wars from 1912 to 1913, but it was his astute military leadership at Gallipoli and the defeat of the Allied invasion that cemented his reputation and gave him the support he needed to organize a*

nationalist revolution in Anatolia and eventually bring down the Ottoman Empire.

In May 1919, Atatürk initiated opposition against the peace agreement imposed on Turkey by the Allies. This opposition was mainly in response to Greek attempts to seize Smyrna, and Atatürk was able to secure a revision of the peace settlement in the Treaty of Lausanne. In 1921, he established a provisional government in Ankara, and the following year, the Ottoman Sultanate was abolished. In 1923, Turkey became a republic with Atatürk as president. Atatürk then established a single party state in Turkey that lasted until 1945. While president, Atatürk introduced social and political reforms to modernize Turkey. These included the introduction of the Western calendar and alphabet, as well as a Western legal system. In his dealings with foreign powers, he strived to remain neutral and maintain friendly relations with Turkey's neighbors. Atatürk died in November 1938, but his influence is still felt throughout Turkey to this day.

Chapter Ten - The Battle of Jutland

The First World War was fought predominantly on the battlefields of the Eastern and Western Fronts, and although there were numerous naval skirmishes and the navy was used to bomb strategic positions like the Dardanelles, there was only one large full-scale naval battle in the First World War. That was the Battle of Jutland, also known as the Battle of the Skagerrak.

The encounter, between the Royal Navy Grand Fleet under the command of Admiral Sir John Jellicoe and the Imperial German Navy High Seas Fleet under the command of Vice Admiral Reinhard Scheer, took place from May 31 to June 1, 1916 near the Skagerrak in the North Sea, approximately 97 kilometers (60 miles) off the west coast of Jutland in Denmark. This was a battle between the two most powerful naval forces of the time and was the only incident in which the British and German dreadnoughts actually fought each other.

Command of the sea was of paramount importance to the Royal Navy. For centuries, the power of the British Empire relied on the premise that as long as they controlled the sea and trade routes remained open the future of Britain was secure. By this reasoning, so long as the German fleet was penned in their ports by a British naval blockade during the First World War, Britain would be safe. The only possible naval threat to the British merchant fleet, which was providing the country with much-needed supplies, would then be the German U-boats, and at this stage of the war, their success had been limited.

Up until the Battle of Jutland, it seemed as though the mightiest naval powers of the day were purposefully avoiding direct confrontation. But in fact, the British were not entirely averse to a battle, provided it took place on the high seas where they believed they had the upper hand due to their superior numbers and firepower. But they certainly did not want to sail directly into the lion's den and engage the Germans in their home waters. Therefore, the British reasoned that as long as they could confine the German High Seas Fleet to port, where it could do no harm, things were best left alone.

The Germans were also well aware of the dangers of a full-scale naval battle with the British on the high seas and had no intention of jeopardizing their fleet. Instead, they kept their ships in port and sent their submarines to harass the shipping lanes and carry out clandestine attacks on the British, hoping to reduce the Grand Fleet one boat at a time. But the submarines failed to achieve their goal, and the Germans were forced to hatch an alternative plan to deal with the Royal Navy. The only way to break the blockade and gain access to the all-important Atlantic was for the German ships to leave the confines and safety of port.

The German plan was to use Vice Admiral Franz Hipper's five fast scouting modern battlecruisers to lure Vice Admiral Sir David Beatty's battlecruisers into the path of the German fleet and thus take them out of the war. Vice Admiral Scheer hoped to destroy Beatty's forces before Jellicoe's Grand Fleet could arrive on the scene. Incidentally, this was the same strategy used by Admiral Lord Nelson at the Battle of Trafalgar fought off the Straits of Gibraltar in

1805. The Germans also stationed submarines across the likely route of the British ships. The British, however, were wise to the German strategy, British codebreakers had been able to intercept German communications and warn the Grand Fleet. As a result, both Beatty and Jellicoe put to sea earlier than the Germans anticipated. On May 30, 1916, Jellicoe sailed with the Grand Fleet and rendezvoused with Beatty, actually passing over the German submarine picket line which was fortunately unprepared and therefore unable to respond. Knowing the German plan, Beatty attempted to use it against them and sent out a smaller fleet on May 31 to lure the Germans into the range of Admiral Jellicoe's main fleet.

The Battle of Jutland was a confused and bloody affair. Late on the afternoon of May 31, Admiral Beatty's smaller fleet, consisting of six battlecruisers and four powerful battleships, crossed paths with Hipper's battlecruisers long before the Germans were ready to engage. The exchange of fire was brief, but in the running battle that ensued, Hipper successfully drew the British vanguard into the path of the German High Seas Fleet, and Beatty lost two battlecruisers. When Beatty observed the High Seas Fleet, which the British had not realized were in the open sea, he withdrew his ships, and the Germans gave chase. This then drew the German ships into the path of the British Grand Fleet. The setting sun on the western horizon backlit the German ships as the two fleets, totaling 250 ships, actively engaged with each other. In this engagement, the Germans damaged Beatty's flagship HMS *Lion* and sank HMS *Indefatigable* and HMS *Queen Mary*, both of which blew up when German shells hit their ammunition magazines.

As darkness fell, Jellicoe, knowing the limitations of his fleet in night fighting, decided not to engage in further direct battle until dawn. But all through the night, he hunted and harassed the German ships and maneuvered his fleet to try and cut them off from their base, hoping to continue the battle when the sun rose again. Jellicoe placed a screen of cruisers and destroyers behind his main battle fleet to patrol the rear as he attempted to cut off Scheer's anticipated escape route. But under the cover of darkness, the German Fleet opted to cross Jellicoe's wake and was able to break through the rearguard and eventually make it back to the safety of the port. Scheer was aided by the fact that the Germans were jamming the British frequencies, and most of the ships in Jellicoe's rearguard were unable to report their separate encounters with the Germans during the night.

Jellicoe and his commanders, therefore, did not realize that the gunfire and explosions that they heard during the night were the German ships breaking through the British lines. They believed that what they were hearing were attacks by German destroyers. Until the early hours of the morning, a chaotic naval battle ensued. Ships got lost in the darkness, coming across each other suddenly and unexpectedly, and both sides suffered significant losses. Several British destroyer flotillas engaged with the German battle fleet throughout the night; five British destroyers sank, but they managed to torpedo the light cruiser SMS *Rostock* (that sank several hours later) and blow up the SMS *Pommern* with all hands lost. HMS *Southampton* was heavily damaged but managed to torpedo SMS *Frauenlob*; she too sank with all hands on board. Shortly before dawn, three British destroyers collided in the chaos, and the German battleship SMS *Nassau* rammed the British destroyer HMS *Spitfire*, but both ships survived the collision and made it back to their respective ports. Finally, at 5:20 a.m., the German High Seas Fleet made it back to the safety of their port.

The Battle of Jutland was inconclusive. The British losses were heavier than the Germans, but the Germans failed to capitalize on their advantage because the battle alarmed both the Kaiser (the king of Germany) and Admiral Scheer to such an extent that they made the decision to return to the safety of port rather than stand and fight. Perhaps it was the British reputation, rather than their superior firepower, that made Admiral Scheer back down when his original plan failed. By the end of the Battle of Jutland, fought over 36 hours, 14 ships from the British Grand Fleet and 11 ships from the German

High Seas Fleet were lost, and a total of 9,823 sailors died in the freezing waters of the North Sea off Jutland. The British had suffered heavier losses than their German counterparts, but they succeeded in cutting off the German High Seas Fleet's bid for freedom and chased them back to port where they contained them for the remainder of the war.

The British had succeeded in their long-term goal of denying the Germans access to the Atlantic, and the Germans never again seriously challenged British control of the North Sea. But because the battle had been indecisive, the threat of the German navy remained, and Britain had to keep their fleet of battleships concentrated in the North Sea, unable to use them in other areas of the war. The Germans' hasty withdrawal back to port, however, did confirm British naval dominance. It reinforced their belief that they were masters of the sea and that the Germans did not want to engage in fleet-to-fleet contact and a full-scale battle between their mighty dreadnought battleships. After a few further unsuccessful attempts by the Germans to reduce the power of the British navy, they were forced to admit that their fleet had been successfully confined to port and subsequently turned their efforts and resources to unrestricted submarine warfare and the destruction of Allied and neutral shipping lanes. This was one of the triggers that drove the United States to declare war on Germany.

The Battle of Jutland was the only true clash of battleships in the First World War and has been recognized as perhaps the largest surface battle in naval history due to the number of battleships and battlecruisers involved. It was also the last major naval battle in world history fought primarily by battleships.

Chapter Eleven - The Decline of the Russian Empire

While France and Britain were bogged down in the trenches of the Western Front, Russia had its own problems to deal with. After the Battle of Tannenberg, the Russian army suffered a series of crushing defeats and continued in a downward spiral, ultimately leading to a decline in morale amongst the troops and the population in general. By the end of 1915, the Eastern Front spanned more than 1,000 miles from the Baltic coast near Riga to the Ukrainian shores of the Black Sea. As the Western Front turned into a stalemate, the Germans became more determined to secure victory on the Eastern Front, and by the end of 1915, they, along with their Austro-Hungarian allies, had driven the Russians out of Poland and Galicia.

In June 1916, the Russians launched a massive counteroffensive designed to divert a considerable number of German troops away from the Western Front and halt their attack on Verdun. One part of this campaign, the Brusilov Offensive, named after Commander Aleksei Brusilov, lasted from June 4 to September 20, 1916 and turned out to be the greatest feat of arms for the Russian Empire in the First World War.

The Brusilov Offensive took place in what is present-day western Ukraine near the towns of Lviv, Kovel, and Lutsk, and was one of the most lethal offenses in the history of warfare. Brusilov effectively used small, specialized units and surprise attacks to break through weak points in the Austro-Hungarian lines, allowing the rest of the army to advance. This was a dramatic change from the usual style of Russian human wave attacks. Its success was based on a combination of good leadership, sound tactics, and unwavering commitment from the lower ranks. Brusilov's offensive was the high point of Russian participation in the war. Unfortunately, the rest of the Russian campaign was dominated by indecisiveness, ineffective supply lines, inadequate equipment, and the use of conventional tactics at great cost to human life (the death toll was estimated to be close to a million), and this destroyed any chance of victory the Russians may have had in the June Offensive of 1916.

While the offensive was ultimately disastrous for Russia, it did, however, help the Allied cause. The offensive coincided with the British attack on the Somme, and these two actions relieved some of the pressure on the French troops at Verdun and on the Western Front as a whole. The offensive also broke the back of the Austro-Hungarian Army, and their estimated losses were approximately 600,000. After the June 1916 Offensive, the Austro-Hungarian Army was increasingly reliant on Germany for military support and resources, placing more strain on the German Army as it now battled to win the war almost single-handedly.

But Russia was crippled by the offensive and was never able to mount another attack on the same scale again during the First World War. The financial and human cost of the campaign also contributed significantly to the downfall of the Russian Empire, as a politically and militarily weakened Russia continued to descend into chaos. The huge cost of the First World War, in terms of both lives and resources, combined with the failure of the overall June Offensive of 1916 severely weakened the already unpopular government of Tsar

Nicholas II and contributed to the rise of communism and the eventual Russian Revolution.

By early 1917, the Russian government was in total disarray, and Russia was on the verge of collapse. In March, widespread rioting and protests broke out in Petrograd, and having lost the support of the army, Tsar Nicholas II was forced to abdicate. This marked the end of the Russian Empire and the 304-year rule of the once mighty Romanov Dynasty. After the abdication of the tsar, a shaky provisional government was established, and despite the collapse of the tsarist government, Russia continued to defend the Eastern Front.

The next significant milestone in Russia's demise was the July Offensive of 1917, also known as the Kerensky Offensive, another unsuccessful Russian military campaign. The campaign was planned by the Russian minister of war, Aleksandr Kerensky, as much for political as military reasons. Kerensky believed a victory would restore discipline to the disintegrating Russian army and rally the Russian people behind the newly formed provisional government. On July 1, 1917, the Russian army, once again under the command of General Brusilov, attacked German forces along a broad front in Galicia. Initially, they were successful, but the Russian soldiers, hungry, exhausted, and demoralized, soon refused to leave the trenches and fight, and by July 16, the offensive had entirely collapsed. The Germans launched a counteroffensive that was met with little resistance.

The timing and conception of Kerensky's offensive were disastrous; it demonstrated how much the Russian army had disintegrated and also the extent to which the provisional government had failed to interpret the revolutionary mood of the people. The Russian population was tired, starving, and disillusioned with the war. It had drained the country's resources, but worse still, it had decimated their population. After the February Revolution that deposed the tsar, popular demands for peace had grown more intense, but as the provisional government continued to honor the alliances made by the imperial government, military discipline disintegrated and unrest grew.

Finally, by November 1917, the population had been pushed to the brink, and the Bolsheviks[1], a faction of the Marxist Russian Social Democratic Labour Party, overthrew the provisional government, seized control of Russia, and began negotiating a peace treaty with Germany. In March 1918, a beleaguered and weakened Russia signed the Treaty of Brest-Litovsk and ended the fighting on the Eastern Front. This may have bought a degree of peace to the region, but the terms of the treaty were harsh and gave the Central Powers control of large amounts of territory in the Baltic States, Poland, and Ukraine.

Russia may have made peace with its neighbors, but there was no peace to be found within its own borders. Shortly after signing the peace treaty with Germany, Russia descended into a bloody civil war. This chaos left the tsar and his family, who had been arrested after the abdication, in a precarious position, and they were held in various locations around the country. The Bolsheviks, fearing that the Imperialists would rally around the royal family to reassert their power, ordered the execution of the Romanovs on July 17, 1918 at Yekaterinburg. This order was almost certainly given by Bolshevik leader Vladimir Lenin.

Russia's three-and-a-half year involvement in the First World War exacted a heavy price. The fighting on the Eastern Front had claimed the lives of between three and four million soldiers and countless civilians. It had destroyed the Romanov Dynasty and left Russia in such political and social turmoil that it ultimately led to the rise of communism.

[1] The Bolsheviks, founded by Vladimir Lenin and Alexander Bogdanov in 1903, were the leaders of the revolutionary working class in Russia and ultimately became the Communist Party of the Soviet Union. The name Bolshevik means "one of the majority." The Bolsheviks gained increasing support from Russian urban workers

and soldiers during the First World War, and this enabled them to overthrow the Russian provisional government in November 1917.

Chapter Twelve – The Battle of Verdun

The Battle of Verdun, fought on the hills north of Verdun-sur-Meuse, dragged on from February 21 to December 18, 1916. This was the longest, costliest, and largest battle of the First World War. In fact, no battle in the history of modern warfare has lasted as long and caused such protracted misery and suffering as the Battle of Verdun.

By the time the Allies and the Germans clashed at Verdun, the war, which many had thought would be over by Christmas 1914, had been slowly grinding away for almost two years with no end in sight. The battle was conceived and planned by the German Chief of General Staff Erick von Falkenhayn with the aim of finally securing victory for the Germans on the Western Front. Von Falkenhayn intended to crush the French 96th Division before they were reinforced by the full deployment of the British forces, as it would be almost impossible for the British to then continue fighting on the Western Front without the support of the French

Von Falkenhayn believed that the war would be won or lost in France, and he felt that a war of attrition was Germany's best hope of victory. He wrote to Kaiser Wilhelm II and expressed his opinion that while Britain was the most formidable of the Allied powers, it could not be attacked directly, and their position at the Somme did not lend itself to a full-scale frontal offensive. He believed that the only way to defeat the British was to defeat her allies. According to Falkenhayn, Russia and the Eastern Front no longer posed the greatest threat, and the Italian Front was not going to play a major role in the outcome of the war, so that left France as the most significant target.

The ancient fortress city of Verdun was not a random choice for the battle. Von Falkenhayn chose this site with care and consideration because he wanted to make a statement. He believed that the key to defeating France lay not in breaking through their lines but rather by attacking a target that they would feel compelled to defend to the bitter end. He wanted to defeat the French at a location where strategic necessity and national pride came together. The fabled citadel of Verdun on the Meuse River offered von Falkenhayn exactly what he was looking for, a salient point in the French defenses.

Losing Verdun would not just have put the French at a strategic disadvantage; it would also have been a huge psychological and moral blow. Verdun was a citadel of immense national importance to the French as it played a crucial role in the defense of France throughout many centuries. After the Franco-Prussian War of 1870, the French built a chain of defenses along their border with Germany, and Verdun was the northernmost fortress of this chain. Von Falkenhayn's battle plan called for the Germans to take the high ground and then use more than 1,200 artillery pieces in a continuous series of limited advances to draw the French reserves into the mincing machine of the German artillery and obliterate them, while minimizing the exposure of the German infantry to battle and limiting German casualties.

The Germans began preparing for their attack on Verdun in January 1916, but fortunately for the French, an intelligence officer discovered the buildup of German troops on the right bank of the Meuse on February 11, 1916. Until then, the French had been focused on planning their own offensive against the Germans, and suddenly they had to turn their full attention to defending Verdun. Over the next ten days, French officers under the command of General Joffre, the victor of Marne, organized a motorized supply chain on an unprecedented scale and used more than 3,000 trucks to move materials, supplies, thousands of troops, and dozens of guns to Verdun to repel the now anticipated German attack. Their hasty preparations to strengthen their defenses at Verdun were completed in the nick of time.

The Battle of Verdun began on the morning of February 21, 1916, with an intense and unprecedented ten-hour artillery bombardment and the steady advance of the German 5th Army. By the end of the first day, the Germans occupied the Bois d'Haumont and penetrated the French defensive lines. The following day, the village of Haumont was razed by artillery fire, and on February 23, the villages of Brabant-sur-Meuse, Wavrille, and Samogneux had all fallen to the Germans. In three days, the Germans had overrun the first line of the French defenses, and thousands of French troops, placed in untenable positions, were lost. As the French were forced back, they bent under the intense German assault, but their lines did not break wide open, and they finally managed to use their artillery to halt part of the German advance at Samogneux.

But still the Germans pressed forward, and on February 24, they took Beaumont, the Bois des Fosses, and the Bois des Caurieres, and advanced toward Douaumont. Only five days into the battle, the German forces under Crown Prince Wilhelm, the eldest son of Kaiser Wilhelm, captured Fort Douaumont, the largest and highest of the nineteen forts protecting Verdun. At this point, the battle appeared to be going the way of the Germans, and the French found themselves under huge pressure, but still they held firm and fought tooth and nail to defend Verdun.

After the fall of Douaumont, General Joffre was replaced by General Philippe Petain. This was when things started to unravel for the Germans, not because of Petain's leadership, but because Crown Prince Wilhelm and his staff deviated from von Falkenhayn's carefully laid plan. Buoyed by success, Crown Prince Wilhelm changed strategy and committed the German 5th Army to greater offensive action. The seizure of ground, rather than strategic targets, now became the priority for the Germans, and by the end of February, casualties on both sides were rising, but little headway was being made. Thousands were sacrificed on both sides to gain little more than a few hundred feet.

General Philippe Petain, who had a well-deserved reputation as a master of defense, brought a fresh army, the French 2nd Army, to fight at Verdun. He was given the formidable task of holding the right bank of the Meuse. The French commanders knew that if the east bank of the Meuse were lost, then all would be lost. If they could not hold this strategic position, then they would not be able to hold Verdun. And if Verdun fell, the effect on morale would be catastrophic, and the French leadership doubted the nation would survive the blow.

Petain's first move was not to push his troops into the vulnerable front trenches but rather to organize them to defend a series of mutually supported strongpoints. He rotated units through the front lines with regularity, ensuring that his troops did not spend long periods of time at the sharp end of the front. Petain also greatly increased the number of artillery pieces at Verdun and subjected the Germans to the same levels of bombardment that the French had been suffering under. And so the Battle of Verdun continued for month after month with neither side being able to turn their successes into outright victory. Backward, forward, the battle raged on and on. Villages were taken one day by the Germans only to be lost again days later. The battle had turned into a bloody stalemate of attack and counterattack.

One of the keys to French survival at Verdun was their ability to keep their troops supplied with ammunition and other vital supplies. Despite constant heavy shelling, the French were able to keep the single road into Verdun, called "Voie Sacree" or the Sacred Way, open and the front supplied with essentials. On March 6, the Germans once again renewed their offensive and attacked the west bank of the Meuse, but this did not break the deadlock, and soon both sides were once again bogged down in their trenches. To add to the misery, conditions worsened as persistent rain fell throughout March and April, turning the battlefield into a quagmire. In late April, General Robert Nivelle took over control of the French forces from Petain and began a large-scale counteroffensive. This allowed the Germans to return to von Falkenhayn's original plan, but it was too late for the strategy to be implemented successfully. In early June, the Germans took Fort Vaux, but this proved to be their last successful attack at Verdun. As each army continued to fight for an advantage, preparations for the offensive at the Somme put pressure on both sides to push for a hasty and conclusive resolution.

By June 15, 66 divisions (approximately 75%) of the French Army had seen action at Verdun. The Germans had only used 43 divisions. The French guns had fired over ten million field artillery rounds, and yet despite this enormous expenditure of resources and horrific loss of life, little had changed on the front, and neither side had made any significant gains. By the summer of 1916, with the British launching an offensive at the Somme, combined with the Russian Brusilov Offensive, the tide began to turn in favor of the French as the Germans were forced to redirect troops to deal with these new threats.

The French 2nd Army finally gained artillery superiority, and this enabled Nivelle to launch a counterattack and retake lost ground. In September, General Charles Mangin, a gifted strategist who held the French defensive line from Fleury to the right bank of the Meuse, proposed a plan to Nivelle that he hoped would liberate Verdun. On October 21, the French initiated their final offensive. The attack started with an artillery barrage across a broad front followed by an infantry assault with three divisions advancing behind a creeping artillery barrage—a tactic whereby artillery shells were fired just in front of advancing lines to aid their progress. By the evening of October 24, the French had retaken Douaumont, and by November 2, they retook the fort at Vaux as well.

In order to exploit their success, the French planned an attack for December 5 with the intention of retaking the entire former second French line that had been lost very early on in the battle. Preparations for the attack began on November 29 with a 750-gun barrage. Bad weather, however, put an end to this assault, delaying the French attack and effectively ending their element of surprise. This gave the Germans the opportunity to launch an aggressive counterattack on December 6. Fortunately for the French, on December 9, the weather turned and what followed was an artillery duel between the two armies.

At 10:00 a.m. on December 15, the final showdown of the Battle of Verdun began, but the Germans launched their counter barrage a few vital minutes too late, and four French divisions were able to attack their lines. By nightfall, the French had captured and destroyed 115 German guns, and more than 9,000 men had been taken prisoner. This engagement, later known as the Battle of Louvemont, ended on December 18 with the capture of Chambrettes. This marked the end of the Battle of Verdun.

Through strategic troop management and the effective use of new tactics, based on specialist infantry sections armed with light machine guns, rifle grenades, mortars, and light field guns, combined with efficient logistics and the resilience of the men in the trenches, the French had finally secured victory. But it came at a tremendous cost. The Germans suffered over 330,000 casualties, and the French lost approximately 370,000 to death and injury.

The landscape of the area has also been forever altered, and nine villages—Beaumont, Bezonvaux, Cumieres, Douaumont, Fleury, Haumont, Louvemont, Ornes, and Vaux—were entirely destroyed. An area covering 170 square kilometers (65 square miles) on the Verdun ridge is declared a red zone due to the presence of unexploded ordnance (unexploded bombs or explosive remnants of war), and it is estimated that over ten million shells remained around Verdun after the battle ended. Forty tons of unexploded munitions are still being removed from the area annually.

The Battle of Verdun also had serious strategic consequences for the remainder of the war. The Allied plan had been to defeat the Germans through a series of large-scale coordinated attacks referred to as the "Big Push," but the Battle of Verdun had inflicted massive damage on the French Army, drastically reducing their number of fighting men. This meant that ultimately Britain would have to lead the "Big Push" on the Western Front.

The Battle of Verdun was one of the longest, bloodiest, and most ferocious battles of the war, and by the time it over, it had decimated both the German and French armies. But the loss was far greater than that for the French, and the scars of the battle on the French national psyche can still be felt to this day. The French will never forget the sacrifices they made to hold Verdun.

Chapter Thirteen - The Battle of the Somme

By the start of 1916, the Allies had had little success on the Western Front, and the war was bogged down in a muddy stalemate of trench warfare. In an attempt to break the deadlock, the Allies developed a plan for a "Big Push" on the Western Front to coincide with Russian attacks on the Eastern Front. They did not choose the most strategic point from which to launch their attack but rather a point in the Allied line where the French and British armies met. And so the Battle of the Somme was conceived.

The initial plan, proposed by the French in early 1916, called for the French Army to lead a Franco-British offensive on either side of the river Somme. They would be supported by the 4th Army of the British Expeditionary Force, but when the Germans attacked at Verdun, the French were forced to divert many of their divisions, and the main attack at the Somme was left in the hands of the British under the command of General Sir Douglas Haig. Haig's plan was for the larger British force to break through in the center while the smaller French Army made diversionary attacks.

At 7:30 a.m. on July 1, 1916, the Battle of the Somme began, and for 141 days (July 1 to November 18, 1916), along a 25-mile (40 km) stretch on both sides of the upper reaches of the River Somme in France, the Allies and the Germans fought a war of attrition. This soon turned into one of the bloodiest battles of the war, and of the approximately three million men who fought on the muddy battlefields, over a million were killed or wounded.

The Battle of the Somme got underway when fourteen infantry divisions of the British 4th Army and five divisions of the French Army, under the command of General Ferdinand Foch, launched their attack against the German 2nd Army. Before the first assault on the German front lines, starting on June 24, the British bombarded the German trenches for seven straight days, firing over 1.5 million shells. Haig expected the bombardment to annihilate the German defenses and destroy their guns, enabling the British to then rush forward and occupy their trenches. To this end, after the intense bombardment, the British ordered 100,000 men over the top. It was an unmitigated disaster.

The British overestimated the effectiveness of their firepower. The Germans had hunkered down deep in their trenches, and the Allied guns had been too thinly spread to achieve their goal; thus, the artillery barrage had failed to knock out all the German guns. As the British soldiers advanced, the Germans retaliated and mowed them down with machine gun fire. The first day of the Somme resulted in 57,470 British casualties, of which 19,240 were deaths, making it the bloodiest day in the history of the British Army. This is a greater number of casualties in one day than the British suffered in the Crimean, Anglo-Boer, and Korean Wars combined. Fortunately, the French, having learned some valuable lessons at Verdun, had more success. The French 6th Army was able to inflict heavy losses on the Germans and only suffered 1,590 casualties. After the first day, several truces were negotiated so that both sides could recover their dead from no man's land. Despite this horrendous start to the British campaign at the Somme, Douglas Haig continued with the attack.

After July 1, despite some advances being made by the Allied forces, the Battle of the Somme turned into another long-drawn-out and bloody battle of attrition so typical of the First World War. Attacks continued throughout the summer, and by the end of the campaign, the Somme offensive included thirteen separate battles.

After the disastrous first day, the British made a series of small attacks over a two-week period. Progress was slow and losses were high, but they kept the Germans under increasing pressure and forced them to divert troops and guns from Verdun to reinforce their lines at the Somme. On July 14, the British attacked Bazentin Ridge. Guns pounded the enemy lines, as, under the cover of darkness, the British soldiers gathered on no man's land and readied themselves for a massive dawn assault. As the sun rose, the British attacked, catching the Germans by surprise; they were able to advance into enemy territory and take the village of Longueval.

On July 15, 3,000 soldiers of the 1st South African brigade occupied Delville Wood (later referred to as Devil's Wood by those who fought there), a key military objective at the Somme. The Germans launched a series of brutal attack on the wood, pounding the area with fierce artillery and machine gun fire, but the South African soldiers held their ground. Even when bad weather turned the wood into little more than a muddy grave, they still refused to retreat, and by the time they were relieved five days later, only 143 men of the original 3,000 were left standing.

Toward the end of July, the Allied troops received reinforcements from the First Anzac Corps. Along with the British, they stormed the village of Pozieres but were met by fierce German counterattacks. For six weeks, the battle raged on as they tried and failed to reach their objective. Australia suffered 12,000 casualties, but they gained no ground.

On September 15, at the Battle of Flers-Courcelette, the British unleashed their new secret weapon on the enemy, the Mark 1 Tank. This was the first time tanks were ever used in battle, but they were still in the early stages of development, and many broke down. Of the 48 tanks, only 21 made it to the battle, and even though the British were able to take High Wood, the troops were too exhausted to make any further progress, and the Allies once again failed to make a significant breakthrough.

Despite making two substantial gains in September, Morval and Thiepval Ridge, the "Big Push" was not really going Britain's way. The deterioration of the weather in October meant that the Allied troops were once again bogged down in muddy battlefields, and the battle against the elements became as significant as the battle against the enemy. The men were exhausted, and every battle sapped their strength and cost more lives. In mid-November, the British launched what was to be their final battle at the Somme, the Battle of Ancre. Here, the creeping barrage was used to great effect, and the British forces were able to storm the German defenses and take Beaucourt.

Despite this success, by the end of the Battle of Ancre, the British realized the futility of continuing with the Battle of the Somme. They were not making the desired headway, so General Haig called an end to the offensive. In 141 days of fierce fighting, the Allies had only advanced 7 miles (12 km), and it had cost them 420,000 casualties. The French had suffered 200,000 casualties, and at least 450,000 Germans were killed or wounded. This truly was a battle of attrition, the futile slaughter of young, able-bodied men.

The Somme was described by a German officer, Captain von Hentig, as "the muddy grave of the German Field Army," and an unidentified German soldier had this to say about the battle: "the tragedy of the Somme battle was that the best soldiers, the stoutest-hearted men were lost; their numbers were replaceable, their spiritual worth never could be."[1]

Today there is a memorial to the missing at Thiepval, and it is inscribed with the names of 72,085 British soldiers who died there but have no known graves. Once this was the site of a beautiful chateau and a picturesque French village, but none of that remains, and now its legacy is as the site of bitter fighting. The memorial stands as a stark reminder of the disastrous first day of the Battle of the Somme, but not far away, on the site of the chateau, is an obelisk that commemorates the capture of Thiepval on September 27, 1916. And even though the Somme is remembered as a futile and fruitless campaign, it was not a total loss for the Allies. Despite the heavy costs, a more professional and effective British Army emerged from the devastation, and many of the tactics developed at the Somme, including the creeping barrage and tank warfare, laid the foundations for Allied success in 1918. The Battle of the Somme also achieved another very important objective: it relieved the pressure on the French at Verdun.

[1] National Army Museum, Battle of the Somme,
https://www.nam.ac.uk/explore/battle-somme

Timeline of the Battles That Made up the Battle of the Somme

First Phase

July 1–13: Battle of Albert

July 14–17: Battle of Bazentin Ridge

July 19–20: Battle of Fromelles

Second Phase

July 14–September 15:   Battle of Delville Wood

July 23–August 7: Battle of Pozieres

September 3–6: Battle of Guillemont

September 9: Battle of Ginchy

Third Phase

September 15–22: Battle of Flers-Courcelette

September 25–28: Battle of Morval

September 26–28: Battle of Thiepval Ridge

October 1–November 11: Battle of the Transloy Ridges

October 1–November 11: Battle of Ancre Heights

November 13–18: Battle of Ancre

Chapter Fourteen - America Joins the War

Europe had been catapulted into war in 1914 with little to no time to consider the implications or consider the consequences. America, on the other hand, debated the matter for two and a half years before entering the fray. At the outbreak of the war, Woodrow Wilson had implored every American to be neutral in both thought and deed, and in the beginning, they did just that. They adopted a policy of neutrality and isolation that lasted until April 1917.

There were many political and social reasons why America wanted to remain neutral or, at least, not actively get involved in the fighting. Woodrow Wilson had won reelection in November 1916 with the campaign slogan, "He Kept Us Out of the War." Besides having ideological reasons for staying out of the conflict, German- and Austrian-born Americans also still remained loyal to their homelands, and the influential Irish-Americans staunchly opposed fighting alongside what they perceived to be the oppressive British Empire.

Woodrow Wilson, a student of modern history, was well aware that the causes of war were not black and white and that the situation in Europe was complicated. He did not believe that it would be to America's advantage to take sides, and as long as America's interests were not threatened and trade could continue unhindered, Wilson saw no reason to get involved in what was, to his way of thinking and that of his supporters, essentially a European problem. America's neutrality extended to a policy of "fairness," meaning that, on paper, American banks could lend money to either side, and trade with both the Allies and Germans was permitted. And in September, the first American Red Cross Mercy Ship was sent to Europe with medical staff and supplies. Appearing neutral and actually being neutral, however, were not the same thing, and Britain's blockade of German ports made trade with Germany almost impossible.

While America may have stayed off the battlefield initially, they did not remain totally unaffected or uninvolved, and they suffered their first casualties on May 7, 1915, when 128 American men, women, and children drowned after a German U-boat torpedoed the British liner *Lusitania*. When this happened, former President Theodore Roosevelt condemned Wilson and his policy of neutrality, calling on America to enter the war on the side of the Allies. But his call to action was unsuccessful. Some Americans, however, could no longer ignore the scale of destruction and devastation taking place on the battlefields of Europe and enlisted to fight in France more than a year before America joined the war. On August 31, 1916, Henry Butters became the first American casualty of the First World War when he was killed at the Somme while fighting for the Allies.

At the beginning of 1917, a chain of events occurred that forced America's hand and brought them into the war. On January 9, 1917, after being battered at the Somme, Germany, fearing they would not be able to win the war by conventional means, announced that they were resuming unrestricted submarine warfare. This was not a direct threat against America but rather an attempt to defeat Britain by cutting off their Atlantic supply lines; however, indirectly, it did threaten the safety of American citizens, especially sailors. As a result, Washington severed diplomatic ties with Berlin. Then in March 1917, a German telegraph, intercepted and decoded by British intelligence, was sent from German Foreign Minister Arthur Zimmerman to the Mexican president, suggesting a military alliance between the two countries. In exchange for support in the war, Mexico would win back Texas, Arizona, and New Mexico if Germany won. When this telegram was made public, there was widespread outrage among the public and politicians alike. As the war moved closer to their doorstep, America could no longer afford to remain uninvolved, and they ended their policy of isolation and neutrality.

On April 2, 1917, President Woodrow Wilson made a request before a joint session of Congress to declare war on Germany. On April 4, the Senate voted to declare war, and two days later, the House agreed. On April 6, 1917, after years of staying out of the conflict, America found itself officially at war with Germany, and within a matter of weeks, the first US troops, commanded by General John J Pershing, were sent to France.

At the outbreak of the First World War, America did not have a large standing army, but with the declaration of war, there was a burst of pro-war enthusiasm, and within a few months, an enormous American army had been mobilized. Soon the American Expeditionary Force (AEF) arrived on the Western Front at the rate of 10,000 men per day, and the war-weary Allied troops enthusiastically welcomed these reinforcements. The fresh troops greatly strengthened the Allied strategic positions and boosted morale. Ultimately, almost two million American soldiers crossed the Atlantic to fight alongside the Allies on the battlefields of Europe.

But it wasn't just boots on the ground that the Allies gained when America joined the war. America also made a major contribution in terms of much-needed raw materials, arms, and supplies. Prior to

America entering the war, the Allies were buying supplies at a cost of over 75 billion dollars a week, but after April 1917, they no longer had to pay this exorbitant amount, and this quite possibly saved Britain and France from bankruptcy. American ships also helped bolster the strength of the naval blockade of Germany.

Chapter Fifteen - The Final Days of the War and the Treaty of Versailles

The Hundred Days Offensive, fought from August 8 to November 11, 1918, was the final offensive of the First World War. The Battle of Amiens marked the beginning of the end of the war. The attack, led by the British 4th Army with men from 10 Allied divisions and more than 500 tanks, broke through the German lines, and by the end of the day, a gap 15 miles (24 km) long had opened up in the German line south of the Somme. The panic sown by the tank attack and the collapse of German morale led General Erich von Ludendorff to refer to the battle as "the black day of the German Army."

The Allies managed to gain 12 miles (19 km) throughout the first three days, and their advance was only slowed because the troops outran their supporting artillery and supply lines. On August 10, the Germans began to pull back toward the Hindenburg Line, a German defensive line from Arras to Laffaux near Soissons on the Aisne. On August 21, Haig launched a fresh offensive at Albert and successfully pushed back the German 2nd Army over a 34-mile (55 km) front. The French then won the Second Battle of Noyon and captured the town of Noyon on August 29 with Bapaume also falling on the same day. With the front line broken, the Allies steadily forced the Germans back toward the Hindenburg Line.

On September 29, 1918, the Allies launched their central attack on the Hindenburg Line, and on that same day, Field Marshall Paul von Hindenburg and General Erich Ludendorff informed Kaiser Wilhelm II that the war was lost and negotiations for peace should begin. By October 5, the Allies had broken through the Hindenburg Line, and on October 8, it collapsed, and the German High Command was forced to accept that the war was over as Germany was on the brink of collapse.

By October 1918, there were mass desertions from the ranks as exhausted and demoralized German soldiers refused to continue fighting. In November, when the High Seas Fleet was ordered to launch a massive attack on the Royal Navy, they mutinied. In Munich, a group of socialists and anarchists seized power, and soon Dusseldorf, Stuttgart, Leipzig, Halle, Osnabrück, and Cologne were all in the hands of Workers' and Soldiers' Councils, and Kaiser Wilhelm II was forced to abdicate and flee Germany.

Even though by September 1918 the defeat of Germany was inevitable, the fighting continued until the bitter end, and sadly the last soldier killed in the First World War was Henry Gunther, an American soldier who died one minute before the armistice came into effect. Just after 5 a.m. on November 11, the armistice was signed between the Allies and Germany at Compiegne in France. On the eleventh hour of the eleventh day of the eleventh month of 1918, after more than four years of suffering, horror, and untold misery, bugles across Europe sounded the end of a devastating war that had left ten million soldiers dead, and the guns finally fell silent in Europe. At last, the war to end all wars was over.

In January 1919, the Paris Peace Conference was convened at Versailles to establish the terms of the peace after the surrender of the Central Powers. Almost thirty nations were present at the Paris Peace Conference, but proceedings were dominated by the "Big Four," namely Britain, France, America, and Italy. Russia was conspicuously absent at the conference. Even though Russia had fought on the side of the Allies until March 1918, when the Bolshevik government signed the Treaty of Brest-Litovsk with Germany to end the fighting on the Eastern Front, the Allies believed they had forfeited their place at the peace table. The Allies also refused to recognize the new Bolshevik government, and they were not invited to the Paris Peace Conference. The Central Powers were also excluded even though it was their fate that was being decided. The French and British called for Germany to be subjected to harsh punitive measures. They not only wanted to punish Germany, but they also wanted to cripple the country and prevent Germany from ever again going to war against them.

The Treaty of Versailles set out the terms of German surrender and laid out the compromises reached at the conference. These included the formation of the League of Nations, reparations, and the honoring of pre-existing agreements regarding the postwar distribution of territories within Europe. Even though it was only the Allied Powers around the negotiating table, discussions were often fraught with tension as each country came to the conference with their own agenda. Britain and France had fought side-by-side for four years with Italy entering the fray a year later, and as America had only entered in 1917, they were not bound by any pre-existing agreements between the Allied Powers.

The first order of business was to carve up German territory, and within the terms of the treaty, the new government of the Weimar Republic had to surrender approximately 10% of its pre-war territory in Europe and all its overseas holdings. The Port of Danzig and the coal-rich Saarland would be administered by the League of Nations. This allowed France to exploit the economic resources of the region until 1935. In the east, Germany lost Upper Silesia, a large section of East Prussia and Memel. This came as a shock to the Germans as they had imagined their borders would be returned to pre-war status. And they didn't fare much better in the west as the Saar was placed under the control of the League of Nations for fifteen years, the left bank of the Rhine was permanently demilitarized, an Anschluss (annexation) of Austria was forbidden, and the entire Rhineland was to be occupied for up to fifteen years. Eupen-Malmedy, a small, predominantly German-speaking region on the border between Belgium and Germany, was handed over to Belgium. President Wilson objected to many of the territorial redistributions that the Allied Powers wanted to enforce, including Italy's demands on the Adriatic, but to no avail, and the Allied Powers redrew the map of Europe to their liking.

Furthermore, the Germans had to accept sole responsibility for the war and pay financial reparations to the Allies to the tune of 132 billion gold Reichmarks (32 billion dollars). This was over and above an initial 5 billion dollar payment and an annual coal reparation of 40 million tons.

The treaty also limited the size of the German army and navy. The army could not exceed 100,000 men, and military aircraft, submarines, and tanks, amongst other weapons, were forbidden. The Allies demanded the surrender of the German High Seas Fleet, but it was scuttled before it reached the naval base at Scapa Flow. Ninety percent of the merchant navy also had to be handed over to the Allies.

Provisions were also made for the trial of Kaiser Wilhelm II and a number of other high-ranking German officials as war criminals. But this never became possible as Queen Wilhelmina of the Netherlands refused to extradite him, and eventually, following two decades as a freeman in exile, Kaiser Wilhelm II died at the age of 82.

The Germans had not expected to be treated so harshly by the Allies, and they soon resented the punitive conditions imposed on them by the Treaty of Versailles, and unrest grew. It would, however, be a mistake to lay the full blame for the Second World War at the door of the Paris Peace Conference, but there is no doubt that the harsh punitive measures imposed on Germany by the Allies played a significant role in the rise of the Third Reich. Adolf Hitler was cleverly able to exploit the economic, social, and political crises of the fledgling Weimar Republic to create the conditions in which he could rise to chancellor in 1933 and ultimately become führer. By trying to prevent another war, the Allies unintentionally created a breeding ground for intense German nationalism that ultimately unleashed an evil force the likes of which the world had never seen before and few could have imagined.

For the Fallen

By Robert Laurence Binyon (1869-1943), published in THE TIMES on September 21, 1914.

With proud thanksgiving, a mother for her children,

England mourns for her dead across the sea.

Flesh of her flesh they were, spirit of her spirit,

Fallen in the cause of the free.

Solemn the drums thrill: Death august and royal

Sings sorrow up into immortal spheres.

There is music in the midst of desolation

And a glory that shines upon our tears.

They went with songs to the battle, they were young,

Straight of limb, true of eye, steady and aglow.

They were staunch to the end against odds uncounted,

They fell with their faces to the foe.

They shall grow not old, as we that are left grow old:

Age shall not weary them, nor the years condemn.

At the going down of the sun and in the morning

We will remember them.

They mingle not with their laughing comrades again;

They sit no more at familiar tables of home;

They have no lot in our labour of the day-time;

They sleep beyond England's foam.

But where our desires are and our hopes profound,

Felt as a well-spring that is hidden from sight,

To the innermost heart of their own land they are known

As the stars are known to the Night;

As the stars that shall be bright when we are dust,

Moving in marches upon the heavenly plain,

As the stars that are starry in the time of our darkness,

To the end, to the end, they remain.

Chapter Sixteen - World Leaders Who Played a Pivotal Role in the First World War

War has been the making and undoing of many a man. And while the identities of the millions of foot soldiers that played a vital role in the war have long been forgotten, the names of the world leaders of this time will forever be remembered for the role they played in the devastation of Europe.

Kaiser Wilhelm II of Germany

Kaiser Wilhelm II, the eldest grandchild of Queen Victoria, was the last German Emperor and King of Prussia. His reign lasted from June 15, 1888, until his abdication on November 9, 1918. To this day, Kaiser Wilhelm and the extent of his role in World War One remains controversial. The general consensus appears to be that he played a pivotal role in the events that led up to the war, but he was an ineffective wartime leader, and once the fighting started, he was largely confined to a more ceremonial role as Field Marshal Paul von Hindenburg and General Erich Ludendorff took control of the army, and in effect, the country.

What is known is that Kaiser Wilhelm II was not a fan of democracy and preferred to rule like an absolute monarch. He resented the social democratic and left-wing movements in Germany and their increasing presence in the Reichstag. He also had a contentious relationship with the British, and there seems to have been no love lost between him and his cousin, King George V. The First Fleet Act of 1898 that initiated the creation of a strong German navy was, at least in part, driven by the Kaiser's desire to build an empire that would outdo Britain in every capacity. Under Kaiser Wilhelm II, the German army became a force to be reckoned with on the political front with generals holding more sway over policy than politicians.

Kaiser Wilhelm II certainly put Germany on a war footing, and when called upon to support the Austro-Hungarian Empire, he did not hesitate. In fact, following the assassination of Archduke Franz Ferdinand in Sarajevo, Wilhelm actively encouraged Austria-Hungary to take an uncompromising stand against the Serbs, effectively writing them what has become known as a "blank cheque" of support in the event of war. It is not known if he realized the chain reaction this would trigger. Or perhaps he thought his blood ties to most of the monarchs in Europe would be enough to avoid a full-scale war. Regardless of what the Kaiser thought or imagined would happen, his encouragement and support of Austria-Hungary certainly contributed to the outbreak of war.

During the war, Kaiser Wilhelm II retained the power to make upper-level changes to the military command, but he was largely a shadow monarch, a useful public relations figure who toured the front lines and handed out medals but made no military decisions, as the true command of the German army lay with his generals. By 1916, Germany had to all intents and purposes become a military dictatorship dominated by the dynamic duo of Generals Paul von Hindenburg and Erich Ludendorff. After his abdication, Kaiser Wilhelm fled to the Netherlands where he lived in exile until his death in 1941. Shortly after the end of the war, the Allies wanted to punish Wilhelm as a war criminal, but Queen Wilhelmina of the

Netherlands refused to extradite him. Following two decades in exile, he died at the age of 82.

Tsar Nicholas II of Russia

After 304 years of Romanov rule in Russia, Nicholas II was destined to be the last tsar. His reign not only ended the rule of the House of Romanov, but it also saw the once mighty Russian Empire decline and crumble as it became a shadow of the great political and military power it had once been. The blame cannot be laid entirely at the feet of Tsar Nicholas II, but as the emperor of Russia and commander of the Russian army during the First World War, he was the face of Imperial Russia and the man the world remembers for plunging his country into turmoil and revolution.

Born near St Petersburg, Nicholas Aleksandrovich Romanov, the eldest son and heir of Tsar Alexander III, succeeded his father to the throne in 1894 and ruled until his forced abdication in March 1917. Shortly after being crowned tsar of Russia, Nicholas married Princess Alexandra of Hesse, and they went on to have four daughters and one son. By all accounts, Tsarina Alexandra was the more dominant personality in the royal family and encouraged Nicholas' more autocratic tendencies. His political enemies called him Nicholas the Bloody because of his violent suppression of the 1905 Russian Revolution, the execution of political opponents, and the Russian defeat in the Russo-Japanese War. He is portrayed by Soviet historians as a weak man and an incompetent leader whose decisions ultimately led to Russia's defeat in the First World War and the death of millions.

Tsar Nicholas II had very little experience of government when he came to the throne, but he was determined that Russia would not be left out of the scramble for power and colonial possessions. To this end, he encouraged Russian expansion into Manchuria, provoking a costly war with Japan in 1904 which ended in defeat. Unfortunately, things didn't improve much for the tsar after that, and in January 1905, on Russia's "Bloody Sunday," the army shot protestors demanding reforms. As opposition grew, Tsar Nicholas II was forced to establish the Duma, or parliament, which gave more middle-class people a voice in government. His concessions, however, were limited, and the secret police continued to crush opposition.

Tsar Nicholas II tried to prevent the outbreak of the First World War, but when all diplomatic efforts failed, he honored his alliance with Serbia and approved the mobilization of the Imperial Russian Army. This gave Germany formal grounds to declare war on Russia. At the start of the war, the position of the monarchy was briefly strengthened, but this did not last long, and Tsar Nicholas II did little to help his cause. By mid-1915, he had taken direct command of the army, but he had neither the experience nor the expertise to run a military campaign, and his decision would prove disastrous for both the nation and his family. With Nicholas leading the army, and therefore often away on military campaigns, Alexandra began to take a more active role in government. This too proved to be an unpopular decision.

Soon, Russia was suffering greatly as a result of the war; there were heavy casualties on the battlefields and rising inflation and food shortages on the home front. Most Russians lived in poverty, and as the war dragged on and the death toll rose, the German-born tsarina became the focus of Russian discontent. As losses on the Eastern Front intensified, it was only a matter of time before things began to fall apart for the tsar as discontent spread and protests erupted around the country. In February 1917, things finally reached a breaking point, and in early March, Tsar Nicholas II was forced to abdicate the throne on behalf of himself and his son, Alexei. The tsar and his family were held captive in various locations before finally being executed by the Bolsheviks at Yekaterinburg on July 17, 1918, putting an end to the once mighty House of Romanov.

History has judged Tsar Nicholas II harshly and blamed him for all of Russia's woes, but he came to power in a time when imperialism was on the decline and the world was in turmoil. By the end of the First World War, Russia was not the only great empire to have been destroyed. Imperial Germany, Austria-Hungary, and the Ottoman Empire were all casualties of the Great War, and by 1919, the face of Europe had changed dramatically.

Georges Clemenceau - Premier of France

As premier of France, Georges Clemenceau declared that he would wage war "to the last quarter hour, for the last quarter hour will be ours."

Georges Clemenceau (September 28, 1841 to November 24, 1929), nicknamed "The Tiger," was a statesman and journalist and French premier during the First World War. Clemenceau was born in Vendee, and from a young age, he was politically aware. Through his father, he met men who were plotting to overthrow Emperor Napoleon III, and later he was involved in publishing newspapers that were closed down for expressing anti-government sentiments. Clemenceau studied medicine before going to America for four years. He was amazed by the freedom of discussion and expression that was enjoyed in America but was unheard of in France. While in America, he taught at a girls' school in Stamford, Connecticut and went on to marry one of his pupils, Mary Plummer. Soon after their marriage, they returned to France, and Clemenceau worked briefly as a doctor in Vendee, but politics was clearly his great passion, so he returned to Paris.

Clemenceau became mayor of the 18th Arrondissement of Paris in 1871, but he soon resigned. In 1876, he was elected to the Chamber of Deputies as the representative of the 18th Arrondissement. In 1880, he started *La Justice*, a newspaper that became the principal mouthpiece of the radicals in Paris. For almost a decade, Clemenceau worked as a journalist and built a reputation as a political critic but refused to stand for office himself. In April 1902, he was eventually persuaded to stand for election as a senator for Var. This was a vital moment in Clemenceau's political career. Once elected to the Senate, Clemenceau became minister of the interior early in 1906, and in October 1906, he became premier for the first time.

During 1907 and 1908, the new entente with England was cemented, but the Clemenceau government fell in July 1909, and he resigned. By 1911, Clemenceau was back in the Senate and was a member of the commissions for foreign affairs and the military. Already, Clemenceau was convinced that Germany was preparing for war and he was concerned that France would be caught off guard, so he made it his mission to find out everything about his country's armaments. When war broke out, he called for more weapons, munitions, and soldiers to be sent to the front and argued for the judicious use of manpower. He also pushed for a more organized and better equipped medical corps.

Despite all his political rhetoric, Clemenceau was above all a patriot, and when called upon to lead his country, he put aside all his other interests, and his sole aim became to win the war. Even before he took over as premier, Clemenceau had recognized that as the war dragged on and the troops got bogged down in the trenches, morale was suffering, and this was undermining the war effort. He made it his mission to create a resolute desire for victory amongst the population of France.

In November 1917, after three years of war and when French morale was at an all-time low, Clemenceau accepted President Raymond Poincare's invitation to head the war government, and this position ultimately earned him the title "Father of Victory." Clemenceau was obsessed with unifying Allied military command, and when he formed his cabinet, he made himself both premier and minister of war. He then convinced the other governments to his way of thinking, and in March 1918, Ferdinand Foch was appointed the overall commander of the Allied forces, and ultimately Clemenceau's strategy proved successful.

On November 11, 1918, the war was finally over, and the Allies signed the armistice with a defeated Germany. Clemenceau then became immersed in the peace-building process and presided over many difficult sessions at the Paris Peace Conference of 1919. He also played an instrumental role in reconciling the interests of France, Britain, and the United States with regards to the Treaty of Versailles and campaigned hard for the disarmament of Germany.

In 1920, Clemenceau was defeated in the presidential election, and as a result, he resigned the premiership and gave up all other political activities. At the age of 80, he took a voyage to India where he went tiger hunting. In November 1922, he visited America where he gave thirty speeches in three weeks, telling audiences that if they forgot that there had been a war, then there would be another. After his trip to America, Clemenceau finally retired to a cottage in Vendee on a dune overlooking the ocean. Even though he had left the world of active politics, he remained extremely interested in world affairs and was concerned about what he saw happening around him. In 1926, he wrote to American President Calvin Coolidge calling for the Allies to unite in the face of German demands. Clemenceau died in Paris in 1929. Fortunately, he never lived to see another war in Europe.

David Lloyd George - Prime Minister of Great Britain

David Lloyd George was prime minister of Britain from 1916 to 1922 and was one of the great reformers of the 20th century. Lloyd George was born in Manchester in 1863, but he grew up in Wales and was a lifelong Welsh nationalist. In 1890, having qualified as a solicitor, he was elected as the Liberal Party member of Parliament for Caernarvon. He went on to hold that same seat until 1945. He had a reputation as a radical and was famous for his opposition to the Anglo-Boer War in South Africa. In 1908, Lloyd George became Chancellor of the Exchequer, and his budget in 1909 provided for social insurance to be partly funded by taxes. The budget was rejected by the House of Lords, but their victory was short-lived as this led directly to the Parliament Act of 1911 that stripped the House of Lords of their power of veto.

At the outbreak of the war, Lloyd George was still Chancellor of the Exchequer, and in 1915, he was appointed Minister of Munitions. In 1916, he became secretary of state for war, but he was becoming increasingly critical of Prime Minister Asquith. In December 1916, with the support of both the Conservative and Labour Party leaders, Lloyd George replaced Asquith as prime minister of Britain. David Lloyd George and his war cabinet met daily, and there were often considerable disagreements in these meetings regarding the course of the war. He frequently argued with Field Marshal Douglas Haig.

Lloyd George felt that Haig was squandering lives, and he was suspicious of his demands for greater freedom of action on the battlefield. Despite his clashes with Haig, Lloyd George was a successful wartime leader who convinced the Royal Navy to introduce the convoy system and supported Clemenceau's call to unify the Allied Military command under French General Ferdinand Foch. As Britain's chief delegate at the Paris Peace Conference in 1919, he was a central figure in the drafting of the Treaty of Versailles.

Lloyd George remained prime minister after the war, and in 1921, he secured the settlement that established the Irish Free State. In October 1922, the Conservative Party withdrew their support from Lloyd George's coalition government in opposition to Britain's foreign policy in Turkey, and Lloyd George resigned as prime minister. He remained in Parliament but no longer held any real power. David Lloyd George died in Wales on March 26, 1945.

Woodrow Wilson - President of the United States of America

Woodrow Wilson, born in Virginia in 1856, was the 28th president of the United States of America and held office from 1913 to 1921. Before becoming president, he was a college professor, university president, and Democratic governor of New Jersey. Once in the White House, he pursued an ambitious and progressive agenda of reform. Wilson was a staunch advocate for democracy and world peace, and at the outbreak of the First World War, he urged the

American people to remain neutral in both thought and deed. Under his leadership, America maintained a policy of isolation and neutrality, permitting trade with both the Allies and Germany until 1917. But by April 1917, America could no longer sit on the sidelines, and Wilson, with the support of the American people and the government, entered the war on the side of the Allies.

On January 8, 1918, Wilson gave his famous Fourteen Points speech to Congress. This speech outlined a potential peace strategy that would end the First World War. He set out the specific goals that he wanted to achieve during and after the war, and in so doing, became the only leader to publicly outline his wartime goals. The fourteenth point on his list was the establishment of a League of Nations to protect the independence of all countries, big and small.

At the end of the war, Wilson played a vital role in the Paris Peace Conference and the drawing up of the Treaty of Versailles. He suffered a paralytic stroke in October 1919 while campaigning for American support of the Treaty of Versailles and was incapacitated for the rest of his term in office. After the First World War, Wilson received the Nobel Prize for his peacemaking efforts, his involvement in the Treaty of Versailles, and the establishment of the League of Nations. Woodrow Wilson died of a stroke on February 3, 1924.

Mustafa Kemal Atatürk - Lieutenant Colonel in the Ottoman Army

Atatürk was the founder and first president of the modern-day Republic of Turkey. Mustafa Kemal, born in 1881, in what was then still the Ottoman Empire, was raised to be a soldier, and his father sent him to military school at the age of twelve. From there, he progressed to the military academy in Constantinople, modern-day Istanbul. He graduated in 1905 and went straight into military service. He fought against the Italians in Libya and in the Balkan Wars from 1912 to 1913, but it was his astute military leadership at Gallipoli and the defeat of the Allied invasion that cemented his reputation and gave him the support he needed to organize a nationalist revolution in Anatolia and eventually bring down the Ottoman Empire.

In May 1919, Atatürk initiated opposition against the peace agreement imposed on Turkey by the Allies. This opposition was mainly in response to Greek attempts to seize Smyrna, and Atatürk was able to secure a revision of the peace settlement in the Treaty of Lausanne. In 1921, he established a provisional government in Ankara, and the following year, the Ottoman Sultanate was abolished. In 1923, Turkey became a republic with Atatürk as president. Atatürk then established a single party state in Turkey that lasted until 1945. While president, Atatürk introduced social and political reforms to modernize Turkey. These included the introduction of the Western calendar and alphabet, as well as a Western legal system. In his dealings with foreign powers, he strived to remain neutral and maintain friendly relations with Turkey's neighbors. Atatürk died in November 1938, but his influence is still felt throughout Turkey to this day.

Paul von Hindenburg – Commander of the German 8th Army

Paul von Hindenburg was commander of the German 8th Army on the Eastern Front in August 1914. He led his troops to victory over the Russian 2nd Army at the Battle of Tannenberg, and he defeated the Russian First Army at the Battle of the Masurian Lakes and successfully pushed the Russians out of East Prussia. For most of the war, he and General Erich Ludendorff took control of the army and, in effect, the country.

Erich Ludendorff – German General

Erich Ludendorff played a key role in ensuring German victory over the Russians at the Battle of Tannenberg. He was less successful on the Western Front though. Ludendorff ordered the resumption of submarine attacks in the Atlantic, an act that helped convince the Americans to enter the war on the side of the Allies.

Erich von Falkenhayn – Chief of the German General Staff

Erich von Falkenhayn was the Chief of the German General Staff from September 1914 to August 29, 1916. He identified and chose Verdun as the battleground on which to attempt to break the French spirit. Von Falkenhayn was commander of the German Army during the Battle of Verdun but was relieved of his command after the Germans failed to take Verdun.

Helmuth von Moltke, Also Known as Helmuth the Younger – Chief of the German General Staff

Helmuth von Moltke was Chief of the German General Staff at the outbreak of the First World War but was replaced in September 1914 after the failure of the First Battle of Marne.

Ferdinand Foch – Marshal of France and Commander-in-Chief of the Allied Armies

Ferdinand Foch was a key figure in the French Army during the First World War. He helped defeat the Germans in the First Battle of Marne. In 1917 he became Chief of the French General Staff, and in 1918 he was appointed Commander-in-Chief of the Allied Armies. He led the Allied troops in the Hundred Days Offensive which finally forced the Germans to surrender.

Philippe Petain – Marshal of France and Commander-in-Chief of the French Forces on the Western Front

Philippe Petain led the French forces at the Battle of Verdun and was hailed as a national hero for repulsing the German attack. In 1917, he was briefly Commander-in-Chief of the French Army, and he was able to improve discipline and raise morale at a crucial time in the war for the Allies.

Joseph Joffre – Marshal of France and Commander-in-Chief of the French Forces on the Western Front

Joseph Joffre, nicknamed Papa Joffre, was Commander-in-Chief of the French forces on the Western Front from the outbreak of the First World War until December 1916. He was hailed by the French as the "Victor of Marne" after France's success at the First Battle of Marne.

Douglas Haig – British Field Marshal

Douglas Haig was Commander-in-Chief of the British Expeditionary Forces for most of the First World War. He took over command from John French in 1915 and led the British forces at the Battle of the Somme and the Battle of Passchendaele

Herbert Kitchener – Secretary of State for War

Herbert Kitchener, 1st Earl Kitchener, was appointed Secretary of State for War at the outbreak of the First World War and was one of the few generals who realized early on that the war would not reach a quick conclusion. As a result, he organized the largest volunteer army the British had ever seen. On June 5, 1916, Kitchener was killed when he was traveling to Russia on the HMS *Hampshire*, as the ship hit a German mine and sank.

Aleksei Brusilov – General of the Imperial Russian Army and Commander of the Russian 8th Army

Aleksei Brusilov, as commander of the Russian 8th Army in Galicia and one of the most innovative generals of the First World War, was responsible for the planning and execution of the Brusilov Offensive in June 1916.

Paul von Rennenkampf – General of the Imperial Russian Army and Commander of the Russian 1st Army

Paul von Rennenkampf was commander of the Russian 1st Army at the Battle of Tannenberg, the first major battle on the Eastern Front at the outbreak of the First World War. After Russia was defeated at the Battle of Lodz, he was dismissed as commander and retired. In 1918, he was approached by the Bolsheviks to serve in the newly formed Russian Red Army, and when he declined, he was shot.

John J. Pershing – Senior United States Army Officer

John Joseph Pershing, nicknamed Black Jack, was a United States Army general who was appointed by President Woodrow Wilson to command the American Expeditionary Force when the United States joined the First World War in April 1917.

Conclusion

The First World War changed the face of Europe dramatically; no country escaped unscathed from the devastation and loss, and even after 100 years, many of the scars remain. Picturesque towns and villages were destroyed, once fertile fields were churned up into muddy quagmires by endless shelling, and these places became the final resting places of millions. Now, memorials to the fallen stand where once there were magnificent chateaux, and rows of vines have been replaced by rows of graves.

The political map of Europe was redrawn. Monarchies that had ruled for centuries were amongst the casualties of the Great War. Mighty empires which had seemed invincible only a few years earlier were destroyed and replaced by republics. And the Allied Powers falsely believed that they had beaten Germany into submission, once and for all.

But the most devastating cost of the war was the human one. Millions of men were killed, disfigured, and wounded. Some recovered, but many never did. They returned to their homes beaten and broken, mere shadows of the strong men they once were. No longer dreaming of honor and glory but rather continuously reliving the nightmare of the trenches, they struggled to come to terms with the horrors they had witnessed. An entire generation of Europe's youth had been sacrificed on the battlefields of the Eastern and Western Fronts in a war to end all wars. But sadly, this was not to be, and twenty years later, Europe once again found itself at the center of a devastating conflict.

Ironically, it was the very desire to avoid war that ultimately led to conflict within Europe again. Hitler's expansionist intentions were already becoming clear in 1936 when German forces reclaimed the Rhineland and two years later annexed Austria. Both these moves were in direct contradiction of the terms of the Treaty of Versailles, and by then it was also clear that Hitler was rearming and building a mighty German air force and navy. But yet the Allies did not put a stop to his aggressive behavior.

In a bid to avoid war, at the Munich Conference in September 1938 British Prime Minister Neville Chamberlain agreed to allow Germany to once again occupy Sudetenland, the German-speaking part of Czechoslovakia. When he returned to Britain, Chamberlain was hailed as a hero for keeping the peace in Europe. But some, like Winston Churchill, who described the Munich Agreement as "an unmitigated disaster," had already seen the writing on the wall. They were, however, not in powerful enough positions to change the course of history. Perhaps if England and France had taken a harder line against German expansion and rearmament, they could have stopped Hitler in his tracks and saved Europe from the misery of another war. But that was not to be, and by the time the Allies realized their mistake, it was too late, and war was inevitable.

It is still hard to imagine that men who had witnessed the utter devastation of the First World War, some of them even fighting on the front lines, had the stomach to do it all again. And yet some did. Men like Hitler and his followers were so determined to see Germany rise from the ashes that they would stop at nothing to achieve their ultimate goal. It seems the only lessons they had learned from the First World War were how to use technology to their advantage and fight more efficiently. At least they avoided the attrition of trench warfare, but the horror that they ultimately unleashed on the world was far more devastating.

Here's another Captivating History book that you might be interested in

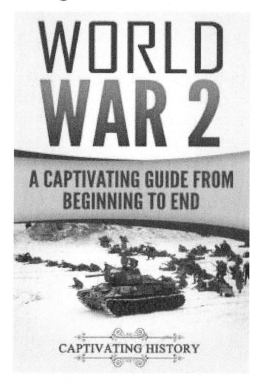

Free Bonus from Captivating History (Available for a Limited time)

Hi History Lovers!

Now you have a chance to join our exclusive history list so you can get your first history ebook for free as well as discounts and a potential to get more history books for free! Simply visit the link below to join.

Captivatinghistory.com/ebook

Also, make sure to follow us on Facebook, Twitter and Youtube by searching for Captivating History.

References

Books and Articles

Carroll, Andrew; Behind the Lines, Revealing and Uncensored Letters from our War-Torn World

Cunningham, Harry; Why Blame the Kaiser? (All About History, Issue 054)

Hart, Peter; Mud; Blood and Gas (BBC History Magazine, July 2017)

Hart, Peter; Bravely battling on (BBC History Magazine, August 2017)

Liulevicius, Vejas; War Land on the Eastern Front: Culture, National Identity, and German Occupation in World War One

Smith, Adam; The Great American U-turn (BBC History Magazine, April 2017)

Websites

https://alphahistory.com/worldwar1/eastern-front/

http://www.bbc.co.uk/history/historic_figures/george_david_lloyd.shtml

http://www.bbc.co.uk/history/historic_figures/nicholas_ii.shtml

http://www.bbc.co.uk/history/historic_figures/wilhelm_kaiser_ii.shtml

http://www.bbc.co.uk/history/historic_figures/wilson_woodrow.shtml

http://www.bbc.co.uk/history/worldwars/wwone/battle_tannenberg.shtml

https://www.bbc.com/news/magazine-31042472

https://www.bbc.com/timelines/ztngxsg

http://biography.yourdictionary.com/nicholas-ii

https://www.britannica.com/biography/David-Lloyd-George

https://www.britannica.com/biography/Franz-Joseph

https://www.britannica.com/biography/Georges-Clemenceau

https://www.britannica.com/biography/Woodrow-Wilson

https://www.britannica.com/event/Battle-of-Tannenberg-World-War-I-1914

https://www.britannica.com/event/Battle-of-Verdun

https://www.britannica.com/event/First-Battle-of-the-Somme

https://www.britannica.com/event/Gallipoli-Campaign

https://www.britannica.com/event/June-Offensive

https://www.britannica.com/event/Second-Battle-of-Ypres

https://chemicalweapons.cenmag.org/first-hand-accounts-of-the-first-chlorine-gas-attack/

https://www.firstworldwar.com/battles/bolimov.htm

https://www.firstworldwar.com/battles/frontiers.htm

https://www.firstworldwar.com/battles/index.htm

https://www.firstworldwar.com/bio/clemenceau.htm

https://www.firstworldwar.com/bio/franzjosef.htm

http://www.greatwar.co.uk/battles/second-ypres-1915/

http://www.greatwar.co.uk/poems/john-mccrae-in-flanders-fields.htm

http://www.greatwar.co.uk/poems/laurence-binyon-for-the-fallen.htm

https://www.history.com/news/10-things-you-may-not-know-about-the-battle-of-verdun

https://www.history.com/this-day-in-history/battle-of-tannenberg-begins

https://www.history.com/this-day-in-history/heavy-casualties-suffered-in-the-battles-of-the-frontiers

https://www.history.com/topics/us-presidents/woodrow-wilson

https://www.history.com/topics/world-war-i/battle-of-gallipoli-

https://www.history.com/topics/world-war-i/battle-of-jutland

https://www.history.com/topics/world-war-i/battle-of-the-somme

https://www.history.com/topics/world-war-i/battle-of-verdun

https://www.history.com/topics/world-war-i/kaiser-wilhelm-ii

https://www.historycrunch.com/second-battle-of-ypres.html#/

1https://www.historyextra.com/period/first-world-war/10-things-you-probably-didnt-know-about-the-bloody-eastern-front-in-1914/

https://www.historylearningsite.co.uk/world-war-one/battles-of-world-war-one/the-battle-of-verdun/

http://www.historynet.com/costliest-battles-and-campaigns-of-world-war-i.htm

https://www.historyonthenet.com/world-war-one-timeline/

https://www.iwm.org.uk/history/5-things-you-need-to-know-about-the-battle-of-the-somme

https://www.iwm.org.uk/history/what-you-need-to-know-about-the-gallipoli-campaign

https://www.iwm.org.uk/history/what-was-the-battle-of-the-somme

https://www.iwm.org.uk/history/what-was-the-battle-of-verdun

https://www.iwm.org.uk/history/who-was-david-lloyd-george

https://learnodo-newtonic.com/nicholas-ii-facts

https://online.norwich.edu/academic-programs/masters/history/resources/articles/6-important-battles-of-world-war-i

https://www.private-prague-guide.com/article/franz-joseph-the-most-beloved-emperor-of-the-habsburg-monarchy/

https://www.poetryfoundation.org/poems/46560/dulce-et-decorum-est

https://www.poetryfoundation.org/poems/47380/in-flanders-fields

https://nzhistory.govt.nz/war/the-gallipoli-campaign/introduction

http://www.richthofen.com/ww1sum2/

https://www.sciencehistory.org/distillations/magazine/a-brief-history-of-chemical-war

https://www.smithsonianmag.com/history/new-view-battle-gallipoli-one-bloodiest-conflicts-world-war-i-180953975/?page=2

https://www.telegraph.co.uk/news/2016/05/31/what-was-the-battle-of-jutland-why-was-it-so-important-to-the-fi/

https://www.theguardian.com/news/2015/apr/24/gallipoli-what-happened-military-disaster-legacy

https://www.theguardian.com/science/blog/2016/sep/16/chlorine-the-gas-of-war-crimes

https://www.thoughtco.com/assassination-of-archduke-franz-ferdinand-p2-1222038

https://www.warmuseum.ca/firstworldwar/history/battles-and-fighting/land-battles/second-ypres/

https://en.wikipedia.org/wiki/Battle_of_Tannenberg

https://en.wikipedia.org/wiki/Battle_of_Verdun

https://en.wikipedia.org/wiki/Christmas_truce

https://en.wikipedia.org/wiki/David_Lloyd_George

https://en.wikipedia.org/wiki/Georges_Clemenceau

https://en.wikipedia.org/wiki/Jutland

https://en.wikipedia.org/wiki/Nicholas_II_of_Russia

https://en.wikipedia.org/wiki/Second_Battle_of_Ypres

https://worldview.stratfor.com/article/world-war-i-retrospective-challenges-eastern-front

Made in the USA
Coppell, TX
06 December 2020